THE FUNDRAISER

THE FUNDRAISER

MEREDITH T. WHITE

NEW DEGREE PRESS

THE FUNDRAISER

ISBN 978-1-64137-961-8 *Paperback*
978-1-64137-785-0 *Kindle Ebook*
978-1-64137-786-7 *Ebook*

This book is dedicated to everyone who has inspired,
challenged, and supported me along the way.

CONTENTS

Choose your corner, pick away at it carefully, intensely, and to the best of your ability, and that way, you might change the world.

—CHARLES EAMES, AMERICAN DESIGNER, ARCHITECT, AND FILMMAKER

INTRODUCTION

I chose to work for John Edwards over Barack Obama in 2007.

If you were paying even the least bit of attention to the presidential race back then, you know I didn't pick the winner and I actually picked an adulterer. But I didn't resign from politics after that campaign evaporated into thin air or go home with my tail between my legs. I had learned too many important lessons, had gotten a taste for the fast pace of politics, and would learn even more in my next decade in political fundraising. But before I share those lessons with you, we have to start in Iowa.

One fall evening on the campaign, I showed up to a Friday night football game wearing my campaign button proudly. I'd front-loaded hours of call time that week to make it to the game with one of my volunteer precinct captains Gayla Sharp and her family. Looking out onto the field, I could recognize a few last names on Centerville High School's jerseys from getting to know their parents that summer. I had just eaten a pork tenderloin sandwich the size of my face, the sweltering Iowa summer had come to an end, and I was still ignorant to the encroaching chill of an Iowa winter. I was full of pork and carbs, and the weather was perfect for football. Sitting in the stands of that rural Iowa high school football stadium was the first time I felt I could thrive working in politics.

Iowa has historically been very important in American politics. In 2007, it had the first open primary on both sides in decades, and at times, ten people were running for president on both sides of the aisle. Competition was fierce. Earning supporters wasn't easy, and keeping them from getting picked off by the other side was a continual challenge. For Democrats, Iowa was going to make or break the campaign.

While working on the John Edwards campaign and spending a lot of time in Centerville, Iowa, my friends were working important jobs in big cities as teachers and nurses. I was crying in my car in small-town Iowa, waiting in the McDonald's drive-through for my breakfast milkshake. To be exact, the car was on loan from my mom.

I was struggling: a combination of culture shock, the fact that this was my first job out of college, loneliness, hard work, and always being either really hot or really cold. As any rundown campaign staffer would tell you, Iowa weather is a lot to handle.

But after an entire summer in Iowa and as my precinct captain proudly introduced me to potential campaign supporters, the work suddenly felt easy. I was in flow. My hard work was paying off.

Before that night, I'd been flailing. I'd been scared of calling strangers. I'd been confused and intimidated by the overwhelming number of moving parts of the campaign. I thought I was missing the whole point and just didn't have what it took. But why?

What I was doing was hard and incredibly time consuming. I was trying to get a community behind an unknown candidate. It took guts and new skills.

My job was scary, and I found no shortcuts to get past the scary parts either. I had to take it one day and one phone call at a time. Then another. Then another. I had to show up. I had to make the calls. I had to make the connections, and I had to face my fears. Once I realized no trick or shortcut existed, it truly got easier. I knew I had it in me to get the job done; I just had to put in the work, and I'd learn what I needed along the way. I felt like I had cracked a code. I hadn't found a missing piece or a failure or even a task in my way. I had found skills I could develop, and that was it.

You can build those skills too.

**

Many of us let fear, complications, and goals get in the way of success, especially in fundraising. Unnecessary complications stop us from making an ask, showing up, and finishing what we set out to do. Anxiety about public speaking, hearing "no," insecurity about what to wear or what to say, failure, and even crippling perfectionism hold us back. How do we ask? Who do we ask? How do we get started? Is our goal even attainable?

Fear is not unfounded. Fundraising, like sales, involves public speaking, talking about money, and potential rejection and embarrassment. None of those rank very high on most people's lists of favorite things. In fact, talking about money is an unspoken faux pas in American culture and even more so for families with inherited wealth, according to the Center for Wealth and Philanthropy at Boston College.[1] More so, according to the Chapman University Survey on Human Fears, public speaking is America's number one fear.[2]

Fears like these aren't limited to the realm of fundraising. Did you ever ask out a crush in high school? What about a raise from your boss? Have you had to ask a friend to pay you back? Or have you ever had to negotiate in a market or argue about how much you owed at a group dinner? Think about your last presentation at school or at work. No one likes risking rejection, but to fundraise, we must get past all these kinds of roadblocks.

The money is out there. Supporters and investors exist. Fundraising still works and so do asking and pitching. Campaigns, startups, and nonprofits are hitting record numbers. According to the FEC, "congressional candidates running in 2017

---

1 Shin, Laura, "The Money Taboo: Why It Exists, Who It Benefits, And How To Navigate It," *Forbes Magazine*, April 14, 2015.

2 Ingraham, Christopher, "America's top fears: Public speaking, heights and bugs," *The Washington Post*, October 30, 2015.

and 2018 collected $1.7 billion and disbursed $1.1 billion."[3] Nearly $28 billion was invested into early-stage startups in 2018.[4] Overall giving grew by 4.1 percent in 2019, which is the sixth consecutive year of growth, and online giving grew by 12.1 percent over the past year.[5,6]

With a few of these statistics and fears in mind, I decided to figure out what made fundraisers unique. What had we conquered? What lessons had we learned to get good at fundraising and get good at it quickly? I didn't grow up in politics, and I sure didn't start in fundraising. I've lost jobs and found jobs; I've almost gotten fired for using Twitter but have also raised millions of dollars with simple emails. I built my skillset while working on winning campaigns—plenty of losing ones too. Working for John Edwards in 2008 instead of Barack Obama (the Edwards campaign offered me health care) was one of the many decisions that would shape my career and lead to my success in fundraising for more than a decade.

But I'm not trying to convince you that fundraising isn't scary. It's full of unknowns. But just like your first day of kindergarten, your first day at a new job, or even a first date, if you understand that no trick, genetic code, secret sauce,

---

3 "Statistical Summary of 18-Month Campaign Activity of the 2017-2018 Election Cycle" *Federal Election Commission*, accessed May 26, 2020.

4 Kate Clark, "Venture capital investment in US companies to hit $100B in 2018," *Tech Crunch*, October 9, 2018.

5 "Nonprofit Fundraising Statistics [Updated for 2020]," Double The Donation, accessed May 26, 2020.

6 "Nonprofit Fundraising Statistics [Updated for 2020]," Double The Donation, accessed May 26, 2020.

or shortcut exists, and instead there are valuable lessons you can learn yourself, then your mindset can transform from unknowing and timid to solidly confident. And with it, your ability to raise money for that cause, campaign, or someone you care about so much will transform too.

Fundraisers are not born; they are built.

**

To supplement my experience and expertise, I've spoken with the world's most successful fundraisers to hear about what skills they've learned or if they were simply extraordinary individuals over the past year. I've spoken to people who have raised millions, some with one dollar at a time, others with six- and seven-figure checks. I've spoken to fundraisers for every type of cause, some of which you might not agree with politically or even know existed.

In this book, you'll read stories about entrepreneurs, nonprofit fundraisers, political fundraisers, coaches, psychologists, consultants, politicos, and even Beyoncé. You'll learn about setting goals, asking for help, showing up, asking for more, making that first call, and what being inside a campaign call time room is like. I'll even take you behind the scenes of the often-hidden world of corporate political action committee (PAC) fundraising. Instead of telling you to work hard, use a few tricks or frameworks, and pick up a phone, we'll delve into all the common roadblocks, how to get past them, and why some aren't roadblocks at all. Fundraising isn't easy, but anyone can do it.

This book is for people who want to make the ask. People who want to fundraise. People who want to learn from experts about taking risks, showing up, and getting started. Now is the time for you to see why fundraising makes sense for everyone and why you can do it too. In this world of overflowing inboxes, mind-numbing content, and frightening political discourse, you have the power to cut through the clutter, to rise above the noise, and raise money for any cause you believe in.

The power of fundraising isn't reserved for the elite in fancy dinner parties in Washington, DC, or for the suave digital strategist. Anyone can raise money for what they believe in, and I'm here to show you how to knock down everything getting in your way.

Now is the time to demystify fundraising.

CHAPTER 1

THE FUNDRAISING FALL

You're a good person and this is just the beginning.

—TAMMY TAYLOR, FRIDAY NIGHT LIGHTS

I fell into fundraising. I was unconscious of my skill set. I think a few other people are unconscious too.

In my second job out of college, I worked as a staff assistant in Senator Claire McCaskill's office. I was still reeling from the John Edwards campaign's folding, and then I failed to get promoted twice. I spent over a year answering phones and speaking to constituents all day long. I had an answer for everything and maneuvered my way around aggressive callers, crazy callers, nonstop callers, and even a few people I knew from home.

"Senator McCaskill's office, this is Meredith," I'd answer for nine hours a day.

"I'm from Alaska and my senator should. . ."

"Oh, hello there, but this is the office of Senator McCaskill of Missouri, not Senator Murkowski of Alaska."

"Well either way, I hate those high gas prices!"

Repeat that same conversation for the multiple female senators at the time with similar last names: Senator Claire McCaskill (D-MO), Senator Barbara Mikulski (D-MD), and Senator Lisa Murkowski (R-AK).

Or consider what you would say to a caller who claims to be a spy, is upset about high gas prices, and is mad about Anheuser-Busch being bought out by InBev. I think I labeled his concern under "intelligence, energy, and small business."

I was the lowest rung on the ladder—unless we had an intern—and I was also the first person you saw when you walked in the office. I worked there when gas prices were skyrocketing, InBev bought Anheuser-Busch, and Obama won his first term as president. It was the best job to get your feet wet on Capitol Hill, and scores of Hill staffers and policy wonks have taken the same path. I was in charge of greeting constituents, scheduling tours, basic research, and guiding lots of Capitol tours too. You showed you were capable and hoped to move up the ladder to the role of a legislative correspondent who helped write the senator's responses to constituents. No one was a staff assistant forever. I thought I knew what I wanted to do next but missed the campaign life too. At the time, I had no idea where fundraising fit in the DC ecosystem.

I tried to do good work, stay organized, give good tours, and most of all, keep tabs on all of the phone calls to the office. It was such different work than fast-paced campaign life. We tracked zip codes and issues and listened to constituents all day. I knew I was doing a good job, but I wasn't conscious of the skills I was refining. After a year there, I wanted to get promoted. The chief of staff and legislative director had another idea.

After those two failed attempts at getting promoted, they pulled me aside and asked if I'd ever considered fundraising. I didn't know what jobs they were talking about or anything about the DC fundraising scene. I had no idea what they saw in me to consider me for fundraising.

The Conscious Competence Ladder explains my confusion.

Developed by Noel Burch, with Gordon Training International, the Conscious Competence Ladder explains the factors affecting our thinking while learning a new skill along four steps through awareness and competence.

Conscious Competence Ladder:

1. Unconsciously unskilled: We don't know we don't have this skill, or we need to learn it.
2. Consciously unskilled: We know we don't have this skill.
3. Consciously skilled: We know we have this skill.
4. Unconsciously skilled: We don't know we have this skill, but we don't focus on it because it's so easy.[7]

---

7 "The Conscious Competence Ladder," *Mind Tools*, accessed May 26, 2020.

When my boss discussed with me why I didn't get promoted, I was already at the fourth step of the Conscious Competence Ladder when it came to quite a few essential fundraising skills. My hours on the phone in Iowa and at the front desk had better prepared me for fundraising than becoming a policy wonk. I just didn't know it.

"You really don't know a stranger. You know everyone. Have you considered a job outside of policy, but in fundraising instead?" they prodded.

"Why not policy?" I replied.

"You're more valuable to us up front talking to strangers than behind a desk in the back of the office. Have you considered a job in political fundraising?" they finally asked.

"No," I responded. "But I will."

At the ripe young age of twenty-three, I guess I thought a shot at getting my foot in the door in Democratic fundraising in DC was worth it, because who knew where it would lead? I pondered whether to take the leap into fundraising and discussed the idea with friends at too many different happy hour locations. I talked to everyone about it, and it was the lobbyist for Anheuser-Busch who ended up helping me get my first interview. That didn't lead to an offer, but they passed along my resume and I was finally hired. I didn't really put the pieces together at the time, but looking back, I was a twenty-three-year-old who spent the entire first two years of her career building relationships with strangers, figuring out their needs, and connecting them to the organization

I represented. Little did I know, I was honing the critical skills for being a fundraiser. I'd been the one calling when I worked on the caucus, but then I switched sides and was the one answering. The perspective helped me learn all the different ways to answer and connect no matter the audience. I was all over the ladder.

Then, one day, a few jobs and a few years later my boss asked if I wanted to be a lobbyist.

I hemmed and hawed for an awkward minute or two. Then he blurted out enthusiastically, "If you wanted to be a lobbyist, you'd be one already. You're a fundraiser."

My heart sank. I hadn't gotten into politics to be a fundraiser.

I had gotten into politics to work on policy. I wanted to change the game and fix the wrongs through legislation and advocacy and action. I had watched the movie *Thank You for Smoking*, a somewhat satirical move about tobacco, firearms, and alcohol lobbyists, and thought, *Now THAT is what I want to do.* Maybe not booze, guns, or cigarettes, but lobbying was what I wanted to do. Building relationships had become my bread and butter and I was in the game, just as a fundraiser and not a lobbyist or policy wonk.

I would keep fundraising in different capacities for the next few years and help senators raise millions of dollars and fight to win reelection. I'd help newcomers pay off campaign debt and invest early in campaigns who had a tough road ahead. I built relationships and learned the ins and outs of political fundraising and lobbying.

Five more years would pass before I realized he was right. I'm a fundraiser. We are still friends today, and he even came to my business school graduation from Georgetown University.

Since then, I have taken on new challenges, a new job, and I show up to work every day to build those essential relationships vital to successful fundraising. I enjoy teaching potential donors about PACs and their mission for our organization. I get energy from signing up a new donor and even more energy working to find another. I'm always learning something new.

I find myself along the different steps of the Conscious Competence Ladder over and over. I'm so glad I fell into fundraising.

No matter how little or how late, the lessons you learn while honing your fundraising skills are valuable even if you don't know it at the time. It took me awhile to figure that out. I found political fundraising as a place where I could use my skills, whether conscious of them or not. You can use your new skills in fundraising to go the extra mile for a charity or level up your ability to ask for what you want. I believe that no matter if you fall into it or not, you can be a fundraiser. You might just not know it yet.

CHAPTER 2

WHAT MAKES A GOOD FUNDRAISER?

Start where you are. Use what you have. Do what you can.

—ARTHUR ASHE

My friend and seasoned fundraiser Gary Whidby learned how to understand his audience while working at Circuit City.

Sarah Blakely, billionaire and founder of Spanx, learned how to take a "no" in stride while selling fax machines.

My time in Iowa taught me plenty about relationships and making an ask.

No single training ground exists for learning the skills to be a good fundraiser.

A good fundraiser can face their fears, navigate roadblocks, and always find in themselves what they need to succeed. Most people assume fundraising is all about money, being an extrovert, transactions, and, what I hear most often, just being born with it.

But what is *IT*?

Most people stereotype and don't know what it takes to be a good fundraiser, which is probably why they aren't fundraisers.

I was wrong too.

However, the skills I've learned throughout my career and more recently through navigating a complicated and at times cumbersome campaign finance puzzle have paid off in funds raised, networks grown, lessons learned, and the ability to face many fears most people live with their whole life. I was not born a fundraiser.

You shouldn't be afraid of fundraising no matter your experience level. It's about so much more—just look at the unofficial job description of my first job as a PAC director. I found it in the depths of my Gmail account from 2014.

"I need a PAC director. Ideal person who is from the Hill or somewhere else in town for a couple of years. Strong interest in politics. Bipartisan outlook. Good writer and researcher. Ability to work in a small office. Well-organized and creative. Interest in attending fundraisers and developing/ maintaining a Hill and broader DC network. I am looking more for an up-and-comer who can grow from the position than an experienced veteran."

Nowhere in there does it say they need to be able to ask people for money. Nowhere does it say they have to be an extrovert or even make cold calls or be a content strategy whiz. Not a single mention of raising money occurs. I had never run a PAC before, and I still got the job.

Have you ever worked retail? Sold Girl Scout cookies? Had a lemonade stand or asked your parents for a later bedtime? You didn't have to have years of sales to make any of those asks and none of them had anything to do with nature or nurture. Without realizing it, you were developing skills critical to fundraising and working on building your skill set to succeed.

No matter where you fit on the introvert-extrovert spectrum, you have a place in fundraising. If you picked up this book, you're on your way. Quit thinking you don't fit the stereotype of a fundraiser.

Sara Blakely used her sales background to help propel Spanx's success: "The cold-calling to sell fax machines was an amazing training ground for hearing 'no.' I just learned that there's a formula. You have to go through a certain number of 'no's to get to a 'yes,' so don't let it discourage you."[8]

Fundraisers hear no a lot. Sara Blakely would be a great fundraiser.

My friend and fellow PAC manager Gary Whidby attests he learned everything he needed to know about fundraising engagement from working at Circuit City for six years and that the "ground rules are largely the same. You have to read your audience, fast, and adjust your message accordingly.... It's all about knowing your audience, what makes them tick, and what makes them give."

Gary and Sarah might be extroverts, but no matter how extroverted or introverted you are, the path to success is lined with the same lessons. Neither personality is better for fundraising.

In fact, many advantages to being an introverted fundraiser exist. My good friend Manjiri Mannino Machak falls smack in the middle of the introvert-extrovert scale. She sees relationships I don't because I'm too busy telling my favorite

---

8 Barbara O'Reilly, "Major Gifts Fundraising 101: It's Not About Us. It's About Them!" *The Non-Profit Marketing Blog*, December 17, 2015.

story. She's slowly amassed millions through thorough research, and I've seen her show potential donors the path to a huge check without even blinking an eye. She's learned to talk to strangers over years and years as a fundraiser and never questioned her skills because she was an introvert. She builds relationships out of thin air. She has the skills to be successful in fundraising, and you can learn those skills too.

According to Barbara O'Reilly, who has over twenty years of fundraising experience, "We are relationship architects between our organizations and the donors who currently or, we hope, will eventually support us. This is true across all kinds of fundraising—annual funds, online/mobile giving, individual and institutional major gifts, events, planned gifts. Our goal is to create two-way conversations that are not transactional and circular exchanges of asking and receiving money."[9]

A good fundraiser knows the work is not just about the transaction but about the relationships. It's about using that drive to show value and make connections where others couldn't. It's about getting past hearing no and understanding your audience. It's your job to help get to the outcome that benefits you and your audience most.

Hank Rosso, the renowned author of *Achieving Excellence in Fundraising*, says, "Fundraising is the gentle art of teaching the joy of giving."[10]

---

9 Barbara O'Reilly, "Major Gifts Fundraising 101: It's Not About Us. It's About Them!" *The Non-Profit Marketing Blog*, December 17, 2015.

10 Eugene R. Tempel, Timothy L. Seiler, and Dwight F. Burlingame, *Achieving Excellence in Fundraising* (Hoboken, NJ: John Wiley & Sons, 2016), 12.

You picked up this book. You have the drive to learn new skills, face your fears, conquer roadblocks, and find in yourself what it takes to be a fundraiser. As long as you have the drive, no matter where you learn—whether it be at Circuit City or not—you can fundraise.

CHAPTER 3

FEAR OF THE NO

Failure is simply the opportunity to begin again, this time more intelligently.

—HENRY FORD

Barack Obama lost his first federal campaign, I've had doors slammed in my face, and I have probably heard no over a million times. If you count simply avoiding a fundraising email, it would be multimillions of nos. I would struggle putting my finger on why hearing no is no longer a deterrent for me. It doesn't faze me.

No! No. No? No. . . . No! No, but no, and, no, uhm.

No is just two letters. It's one word. It can be a one-word sentence. It is an answer and sometimes a question. So many different ways to say it. My favorite is the *no, but*, or the *no?* The fear of hearing a no when fundraising is wrapped up in rejection, failure, and disappointment. A no isn't just the feelings you get when you hear it. It's the facial expressions, the curt response, the easy way out. It's a furrowed brow or an exasperated breath before you even get to explain yourself or why you're reaching out. Rejection isn't easy, but it's one of the best ways to gain confidence and take advantage of the opportunities in front of you.

When I was just over a year into PAC fundraising, I was working an event at a nice hotel in Arizona. I knew everyone at this event could afford to contribute to the PAC. and I had done quite well at similar events in the past. I had my contribution forms, my wedge heels for walking around the immaculately manicured garden courtyard, my bold, patterned, preppy, and work-appropriate dress, a handful of pens in my purse, and a list with every attendee. I felt confident I'd come home with new donors and self-sufficiency.

But they had changed the format entirely. I was used to consistent traffic at break times, which felt like fishing in a barrel. I knew the best times to fundraise, where to stand, and even when to get coffee. This time there were seated tables and no kiosks for my home base or even for conference attendees to come find me later. They had nixed kiosks altogether, and I could only network at mealtime or cocktail hour. There was no hallway traffic or even bottleneck to take advantage of in front of the coffee and snack bar. All of these little details changed my flagrant confidence into cautious—and a bit timid— optimism. Over the past few years, I'd built up a history of success at these events. This new format meant any and all fundraising I would do was going to be via networking at events where funding a PAC or worrying about politics was the last thing everyone wanted to think about. Starting conversations with strangers wasn't hard at big networking events but was a million times easier with a kiosk. I had a history of coming back from these trips with a handful of new contributions and none of my own business cards left. It was a beautiful way to fundraise, and sometimes I even got a tan. But this time I was very wrong.

I got one no after another. One attendee's wife even glared at my name tag, "Political Affairs Manager," shining brightly under my name on my magnetic name tag and looked at me deadpan and asked, "Why are you here?" Others avoided me after they learned I was there to fundraise. I didn't even have a table assignment, so it felt like an unwelcoming middle school cafeteria filled with unnecessary judgement and entitlement. That feeling of no safe landing or home base was nauseating. I had avoided my middle school cafeteria every day in eighth grade by working on an independent project in the computer lab and avoided that feeling at all costs. I had heard no before at these types of events so I wasn't afraid of rejection, but in prior years I had always had a next person to ask, another target around the corner, because the kiosks attracted potential donors like flies especially if my boss was there with me. But this time I came back with no contributions. I felt like a failure.

But failure is normal. Failure is a part of success. Not many people know more about success and failure than Soichiro Honda, founder of Honda Motor Company, who said, "Success can be achieved only through repeated failure and introspection. In fact, success represents 1 percent of your work, which results only from the 99 percent that is called failure."[11]

---

11 Startup.com LLC, "Startup Failure: It Happens. Let's Talk About It," accessed May 26, 2020.

He faced many roadblocks along the way to founding his successful company we know today. He started as a race car driver, but his career ended when he was thrown from his car at the finish line and severely injured his left eye. His career ended then and there. Did you know he founded his company because his piston rings were turned down by Toyota? Later, and multiple times, his plant was partially destroyed during the Second World War and a fuel shortage inspired his motorbike development.[12]

I didn't found Honda Motor Company, but I did bounce back at that conference from the lack of my safety blanket kiosk. I had to get okay with a new situation, new struggles, and new ways my potential donors could and were saying no. I had to realize I was more than prepared to keep fundraising to the best of my ability. I focused on creating better relationships with the people I did know. I made a game of it and was determined to find out the names of the children everyone I knew. I worked to meet potential donors' wives. I asked more questions and learned more. I heard more than a fair share of nos and was brushed off almost immediately from some attendees, but I was okay with it because I was learning and getting better at my craft. I knew I'd be fine; I was learning and getting tougher with every new interaction.

You have to be okay with hearing no. You have to be okay with feeling rejection and hitting a roadblock. It's a part of the process. You can get there. You just have to do the work. You have to build a mindset.

---

12 Josh Bauerle, "Lessons in Overcoming Obstacles From Honda Motor Company," *CPA on Fire*, accessed May 26, 2020.

HEARING NO STRENGTHENS YOUR MINDSET.

Former President Barack Obama lost his first federal election to Bobby Rush in 2000. Obama had been serving in the Illinois State Senate since 1996 and only received 30 percent of the vote to Rush's 60 percent.[13] In that race, Bobby Rush had name recognition at 90 percent, while Obama had just 11 percent. Bobby Rush's son died mid-campaign and the legislature had a special session to vote on gun safety, an issue important to Rush. Obama missed a vote in the Illinois State Senate when he left for Christmas holiday with his family in Hawaii and was put through the wringer for it in the press. The *Chicago Tribune* characterized those who missed the vote as "a bunch of gutless sheep." Obama lost the race, but he didn't let it end his political career—he grew from it.[14]

According to NPR's Don Gonyea, "Even in losing, Obama gained plenty in losing to Rush. He vastly improved his name recognition. He made political friends and gained fundraising experience. And he ran a relatively positive campaign, emerging without having burned any political bridges."[15] Instead of seeing his loss as a failure, Obama saw it as a moment of growth. He could have stopped there, but instead he took this as an opportunity. Failure is the most common and richest source of growth and learning.

---

13 Janny Scott, "In 2000, a Streetwise Veteran Schooled a Bold Young Obama," *New York Times*, September 9, 2017.

14 Janny Scott, "In 2000, a Streetwise Veteran Schooled a Bold Young Obama," *New York Times*, September 9, 2017.

15 Don Geyea, "Obama's Loss May Have Aided White House Bid," *NPR*, September 19, 2007.

Abner J. Mikva, a former congressman and supporter of Obama, even called him a "very apt student of his own mistakes."[16]

Obama strengthened his mindset. Obama must've been scared. He knew it could happen all over again. He must've remembered and even dwelled on what they said in the press. But thankfully, he was a student of his own mistakes and his mindset wasn't fixed in place, or else he never would have run for office again.

According to Carol Dweck, PhD, "In a fixed mindset, people believe their basic qualities, like their intelligence or talent, are simply fixed traits. They spend their time documenting their intelligence or talent instead of developing them. . . . In a growth mindset, people believe that their most basic abilities can be developed through dedication and hard work—brains and talent are just the starting point."[17]

A growth mindset keeps going even in the face of rejection. Over the years, I've gained confidence through failures and learned I can always develop my talents and keep learning. I got better at networking and crafting my ask. I couldn't get better if I'd stopped once I failed.

Lots of failure goes unnoticed on the way to success. It's the only way to get there. But your hard-earned mindset will help you along the way. A fixed mindset was not any

---

16 Janny Scott, "In 2000, a Streetwise Veteran Schooled a Bold Young Obama," *New York Times*, September 9, 2017.

17 Great Schools Partnership, "GROWTH MINDSET," accessed May 26, 2020.

part of Barack Obama's successful campaign for president. If so, he never would have been able to walk hand in hand with his wife and daughters to accept the nomination as the first African American president in history. He grew from a confident young politician facing a blowing loss to winning the Senate and then presidency with a historic turnout. I'm so glad he did.

NEVER WASTE A NO.

Consistently, fundraisers I spoke with viewed a no as an opportunity to pivot.

You can glean so much information from a no—so much opportunity.

It makes sense to fear rejection, but would you be similarly afraid of an opportunity? Of an open door? What if I told you I have no fear of hearing no when I send a fundraising email or make a fundraising call? I don't see nos as rejections anymore. I see them as an opportunity to learn more about how to get a yes next time and how to better aim for my goals.

In door-to-door canvassing, you're taught to ask about issues important to a potential voter or caucus-goer, even if they are not a fan of your candidate. It helps you pivot the conversation and also learn more about them and how to follow up. A way to pivot is always there. In 2007, we didn't have smartphones or tablets, but instead clipboards and Google Maps. Those clipboards had all of my target doors to knock, with names and top issues they cared about along with any notes left by a previous canvasser. Those notes helped me pivot especially if I heard an "I don't know." Even bundled up in my L.L. Bean jacket from high school, wearing at least five layers of clothes and fumbling with my gloves to write down more info on those clipboards, I knew I couldn't waste any information from those encounters, even if some people wouldn't let me past their screen door.

I found out about events I never would have known about. I met people's sisters and aunts and uncles and knew who was a baker or a chiropractor and who could help remind their neighbor to caucus. Those bakers helped supply breakfast for a busload of journalists days before the caucus. The chiropractor had an office downtown I could use as a satellite office, and I saw neighbors walk to the caucus together on caucus night. If I'd simply heard yes at every door, I never would have learned so much about the community and how to connect with it.

A good friend of mine and veteran nonprofit fundraiser Sterling Morriss Howard explains how hearing no helps her in fundraising:

> "Asking why or other follow up questions in response to a no can give you vital donor information to use in future asks. For example, was the timing of the ask wrong because this donor has already made their charitable decisions for the year? Was the

amount of the ask wrong because you underestimated how much the donor is already giving elsewhere? Does the donor not feel connected enough to what you're doing? When you get a no, you should try to find out the answers to questions like this. Then, you can better tailor your ask next time. It's a chance to do it better."

The more rejections you face and nos you hear, the more chances you have to get better and learn more and more. The work is not solely a numbers game, but you have to hear no to get better at hearing no and find the benefits hidden within it.

CHAPTER 4

FEAR OF THE ASK

I love fear. Fear sets me free. Bring it on.

—COMEDIAN NIKKI GLASER

How do you ask for money, and why is it so scary to most people? It's a crippling fear. But an ask is only a question. It can also be a request, an encouragement, or a guided hand to involvement in something more. You've probably asked for more things than you realize. Over the years your asks have gotten more complicated: an ask for food, candy, or a new toy; an ask to go play on the playground, to start something new, to watch the tv show you want to watch, or to listen to the music you want to listen to; and asking out a crush, asking for a raise, asking for more beer, asking for coffee, or an invitation to an event. You've made an ask already.

Since one hundred percent of contributions are the direct result of an ask, what's holding you back?

Fear is holding you back.

But it makes sense to be afraid to ask for money, especially when your favorite cause or job is on the line. When it comes to asking for a contribution, I'm your girl. This is because I've worked through the fear of the ask. I trust what I've learned. I've swum in the depths of fearing rejection and came out alive. Every candidate for office from school board to president, every startup founder, and every development professional has faced the fear of asking for money.

Despite what people say, no exact way to ask exists, and no script that will guarantee victory. At the end of the day, an ask is just an ask.

To get past the fear, let's take a look at four realizations I've gleaned from years and years of honing my own ask.

EVERY ASK GETS EASIER.

The first time I had to ask for a PAC contribution, I fumbled and avoided the ask with all my might. I had to raise funds from employees to support our federal political action committee, which in turn supported the campaigns for reelection of incumbent members of Congress. This was the first time I had to ask for a contribution in person. I'd done it on the phone before, but face to face is different, especially at a kiosk. Yes, you can read their facial expressions, but you can also see them look away to find an escape route. You might even be mistaken for event staff if you wear black. You can't stop to think, so you must be concise to make your point. It's like an elevator and sales pitch in one. Once, I thought I had someone interested, but they ended up asking for directions to the bathroom. That was the last time I wore all black to a conference.

I was in Miami at a kiosk in a giant convention area at a huge hotel on the beach. My palms were sweaty, and I'd already had four cups of coffee. I'd perfected my approachable-but-put-together DC look of a brightly colored work dress and a navy Brooks Brothers blazer. I never wear this anymore, but back then it was my jam. I kept straightening the papers on the kiosk. My current boss was standing next to me throughout the whole endeavor. He heard every try, every avoided explanation, and every step closer to the ask. I kept talking to people, and I kept failing. But I kept trying.

And the more you try, the easier it gets.

Take a look at professional basketball player Steph Curry and his pregame routine. Curry takes at least 150 shots before a game. Does he do it because it's easy? Does he do it because it's fun? Maybe. Does he do it because it helps prepare him to start a professional basketball game? Definitely. He's practiced his shot over 150 times. Practicing helps him get focused. During his warm-up he's already tried and failed, so by tipoff, he's ready.

Trying something out in order to lessen the fear involved is actually an adaptive advantage for all humans. Noam Shpancer, PhD, who specializes in adult anxiety disorders, explains, "Habituation, defined formally, refers to the fact that nervous system arousal decreases on repeated exposure to the same stimulus. In layman's terms, it means that familiar things get boring."

Once you try and fail enough times, the act of asking for a contribution doesn't faze you. It has become a boring task. It's boring and easy and keeps getting easier. But if you avoid it, it will lurk around every corner as a fear you've never faced.

According to Shpancer, "When you avoid something that scares you, you tend to experience a sense of failure. . . . Finally, avoidance eliminates practice. Without practice, it is difficult to gain mastery. Without mastery, confidence is less likely to rise."[18]

To survive that big ask, you have to start asking and keep asking. It took me three days of asking this way and that and warming up at breakfast by talking to strangers before I finally got my first PAC donor.

That time in Miami, when I got the new donor's contribution form, I looked at my boss. He was beaming. I would end up getting more donors that trip and in the trips to come. That first one was the hardest, but if I hadn't kept asking, it would've never gotten easier. I didn't have a hidden talent. I learned how to do it and did it enough to make it inconsequential. An ask will always be just an ask, so get going.

THE FIRST ASK WILL EMPOWER YOU TO MAKE ANOTHER.

You can slowly learn to turn off fear, but you have to start somewhere. Start with the first ask. Revel in the opportunity

18 Heather Edwards, "Overcoming Fear: The Only Way Out is Through," *Psychology Today*, January 7, 2015.

and accept that you will fumble. Those fumbles will help you get that first yes, which will give you more strength than you've ever imagined.

Each first ask has empowered me to ask again. As a candidate fundraiser, I would prepare calls for our clients. Senators would call to ask different individuals, corporations, or associations—you name it—to host fundraising events in town while the Senate was in session. We often targeted PAC money from corporations or affiliated groups or companies with a large presence or stake in the senators' home states.

The first time one of my targets resulted in a YES was a jolt of electricity.

That year, I helped keep the company running while my boss had been out on maternity leave. I wasn't fearless; I had only learned to turn off my fear. I was scared because I was young and had only recently learned how to fundraise. I had a lot of responsibility in my hands and a lot of opportunity I didn't want to waste on being scared.

Scott Lilienfeld, a professor of psychology at Emory University, tells us the secret of people who are capable of facing their fears: "They are heroic not necessarily because they are constitutionally fearless, but because they can learn to turn their fear off."[19]

---

19 Heather Edwards, "Overcoming Fear: The Only Way Out is Through," *Psychology Today*, January 7, 2015.

The ability to turn my fear off helped me when I was still getting my feet wet at my most recent job. I made an ask almost as soon as I walked in the door. I pulled off the Band-Aid because I knew the longer I waited, the more the fear would build up. Turn off that fear as soon as possible.

Let's take a look at the facts: Studies have shown that one of the most common reasons donors contribute is simply because they were asked. Donors want to be asked, so flip that off switch.[20]

Once, along with the rest of the team, I was invited to meet a firm executive who was visiting. The team had to get to know the executives in case they came back to town or had to interact with government officials. I was new to the team, and when my turn to talk was up, I accidentally introduced myself as the PAC manager at my former employer instead of the employer I was currently representing. My face turned red, but then I asked, "Why don't you give to the PAC?" My bosses breathed in audibly and started to awkwardly laugh to ease the tension. I stayed the course and asked for more information, more intel; I asked and asked. A week later we got a check in the mail from this same executive—his very first contribution. He'd never been asked.

ONE ASK LEADS TO THE NEXT.

Political fundraisers aren't the only ones making awkward asks. Wendy Kopp, founder of Teach for America, made her

20 Michael Sanders and Francesca Tamma, "The science behind why people give money to charity," The Guardian, March 23, 2015.

fair share of awkward asks too. In the beginning, she was desperate for funders.

The year was 1989, and Kickstarter didn't exist; neither did Facebook, Gmail, Salesforce, or any of the other online tools so many fundraising shops use today. Some people would've used that as an excuse not to start. How could they, without access to any fancy online tools? Wendy Kopp started with the development office at her university. A news article inspired her, and she ended up in Ross Perot's office.

Asking will lead to your next opportunity, so be ready for what's next.

My friend Manjiri Mannino Machak, a veteran fundraiser in her own right, proclaims, "Just make the ask—it's not that hard. If you're calling them, they have the money. They need to be taught how to give it away and they need a reason to get rid of it. You need to be that reason they part with their money."

Wendy Kopp figured out how to be the reason. When she finally got Ross Perot to be a donor, she didn't miss a beat. She knew his involvement and investment in her cause would legitimize her next asks.

It all started from her senior thesis, the idea she believed in from the beginning. She wouldn't have gotten anywhere if she'd merely written that thesis and hoped for an A. She made those first calls and wrote those first letters, and in fundraising, sometimes that's the hardest part. Finally, she landed in Ross Perot's office.

Wendy Kopp recounts Perot's exciting words in Guy Raz's NPR podcast *How I Built This*: "And he said, I'll tell you what, I will give you $500,000 if you can raise the other 1.5 million. And that was the moment I knew it's done. Like I knew that his credibility and that kind of leverage. I could just go back to everyone else and that they would all come in."[21]

Teach for America started with a goal of a $2.5-million budget and now operates at around a $300-million budget with seven to eight thousand teachers in schools at any time and a thriving alumni network of fifty thousand people, many of whom are still in the public education system. Wendy was ready to hit the ground running after solidifying her largest donor instead of resting on her laurels. She kept asking; she faced her fears and kept going.

MAKING THE ASK HELPS EVERYONE INVOLVED.

Making the ask not only helps the cause, but it also shows others that failure and fear are part of the process. When I first arrived in Iowa for the 2008 Iowa caucus, I was on my own. I needed volunteers, I needed supporters, but I also needed a place to make calls, a place to work late, and even a place to stay some nights. I needed a lot. I had to ask for a lot. But the further I got in the campaign, the less the work was about getting a direct result from my ask. Instead, it was about making that awkward ask so others would too; I had to put myself on the line so more people would show up, caucus for my candidate, and get involved in the campaign.

---

21 Wendy Kopp and Guy Raz, "Teach For America: Wendy Kopp," July 8, 2019, in *How I Built This*, produced by NPR, podcast, MP3 audio, 20:38.

I learned that making an awkward ask is usually the most direct way to get people involved. It's not a risk; it's just an ask. It is often confused with asking for too much, using up chips, and being rude. Actually, many people see it as a positive opportunity.

Former fundraiser and serial startup employee Joshua Hone explained to me, "The most important misconception about asking for help/advice/introductions: Folks are nervous, thinking you are burning political capital or asking someone else to do so. More often than not, getting involved in something exciting (a startup, a nonprofit effort, a political cause) is something that will be remembered positively and not the other way around."

Once, one of my volunteers even invited me to family dinner. I have benefited again and again from simply asking.

On another occasion, I got a high school senior to use his car in a parade. Another person would house three high school volunteers I had recruited from my hometown, feed all of us, and then host a Breakfast Bus Tour stop for the campaign at 5:00 a.m. Putting myself out there showed me that the awkward ask always releases unexpected benefits. All I had to do was ask.

A local campaign precinct captain and the 5:00 a.m. event host Debbie Kury said to me, "I am still getting comments about the breakfast. People are saying they saw it in the paper and on TV. There is someone new that mentions it almost every day. I tell them I had the most fun that week that I have had in long time."

Whether for campaigns or startups, the ask is what leads to the future. It leads to the next investment. It leads to the next contribution, and it can lead to your next success, or even your next breakfast. So get started.

CHAPTER 5

FEAR OF THE AUDIENCE

We're building something, here, Detective, we're building it from scratch. All the pieces matter.

—LESTER FREAMON, *THE WIRE*

If you are going to raise money, you have to have someone to raise it from. This is often one of the biggest roadblocks for fundraisers. You're not just building an audience, you're building connections. If you do it right, the audience will grow itself. Connection is everything. Before you can grow your audience, you need to know them, you need to know whom you want to target, understand, and help.

Your audience matters. I want to show you the importance of understanding, growing, and even refining your audience. Successful fundraising is all about connection.

MAKE THE CONNECTION EASY FOR YOUR AUDIENCE.

The most successful salesmen make you feel like one hundred bucks, the most successful fundraisers make you feel like you can save the world, and the best startups make you feel like your investment will change the way the universe works. These salesmen, fundraisers, and startup employees have figured out a way to connect you to a cause and make you feel like you can do something about it. They figured out the connection. You're building something. All the pieces matter.

I've gotten some of the best sales from Robert California, a fictional character from the hit television show *The Office.*

Robert California put his sales advice bluntly: "You see, I sit across from a man. I see his face. I see his eyes. Now does it matter if he wants a hundred dollars' worth of paper or a hundred million dollars of deep-sea fishing equipment? Don't be a fool. He wants respect. He wants love. He wants to be younger. He wants to be attractive. There is no such thing as a product. Don't ever think there is."[22]

The Office is a fan favorite in my house. My husband convinced me to watch it. I, on the other hand, am still on a mission to get everyone I know to watch *Friday Night Lights.* When you try to convince someone to watch a television show, without realizing, you curate how you describe the show based on whom you were trying to convince. Let's take *Friday Night Lights.* If you were trying to get your friend who is a fan of football to watch *Friday Night Lights,* would you also mention the family drama and emotional scenes? Probably not. You'd mention the swirling camera shots of bone-crunching tackles and the almost spiritual nature of

---

22 *The Office,* season 7, episode 10, "Search Committee," directed by Jeffrey Blitz, aired March 19, 2011, on NBC.

high school football in small-town Texas. What if you were trying to convince your movie snob friend? Maybe you'd mention the incredible character growth and emerging stars and familiar faces. Instead of simply saying, "You should watch it," you made it easier for them to find a connection to the show and take a chance. You could make it even easier by giving them your Netflix password, but that's up to you.

By making the connection to the potential television shows, you let your audience decide and simply led the way.

I once used these lessons to prod a potential donor so I could secure a donation for the PAC for which I was manning a kiosk at a sunny location in the depths of a giant hotel. I had on comfortable shoes because I knew I'd be standing all day and was wearing bright colors so no one thought I was staffing the event. A bigger guy approached my table with his brow already furrowed. PACs can evoke a lot of assumptions and frustrations with politics because many people don't understand the functions of PACs, and when they find out a new way money is involved, it knocks them off kilter. At least one angry individual always singles me out as the embodiment of all that's wrong with politics. And sure enough, here he was—that naysayer marching across that beautiful lobby straight toward me. He came to tell me he didn't like politics and he wanted to keep it as far away from his work as possible. He told me he was just fine being a dad and having a job without being involved in the whole political mess. Talk about privilege.

I had to find a connection, so I went with the easiest one first: family. Did he have a daughter or son or a wife? Did they go to school? Private or public? Did he like bringing his wife on this trip and was he happy with how his job provided for this family? I had made the connection between what happens in DC and the legislation affecting his work immediately by connecting it to his ability to provide for his family. His work provided a respectable place on boards and in his community, and he had pride in this. I made him realize how important his work was to him and his family, and how it provided him a sense of belonging. I then showed him how his contribution to this PAC would help keep safe that sense of belonging and respect because we'd be working to maintain or even make it better for him. He joined right there on the spot—I had simply led the way.

In one of my favorite books on human interaction, *How to Win Friends and Influence People*, author Dale Carnegie explains the success of this interaction, "No one likes to feel that he or she is being sold something or told to do a thing. We much prefer to feel that we are buying of our own accord or acting on our own ideas. We like to be consulted about our wishes, our wants, our thoughts."[23]

I wasn't convincing the political naysayer to join the PAC by force but instead by helping him make the decision on his own. I wasn't setting up Netflix for friends so they could watch *Friday Night Lights* but instead I was explaining how they could relate to it themselves.

---

23 Dale Carnegie, *How to Win Friends and Influence People* (New York, NY: Pocket Books, 1981), 156.

Psychologists have found that humans are not hardwired with their own self-beliefs either, meaning you don't have to find the exact people who love your cause right off the bat. Instead, you can find people who could be socially influenced to get behind your cause too—all in support of social harmony.

We are all predisposed to strive to fit in socially with those around us. We can use this not only to make new friends, but to earn supporters for a cause we believe in and identify investors too. It's just up to you to make it as easy as possible.[24]

Whether frazzled and grabbing coffee or with a chest puffed up, ready for a political debate, connection moves the conversation forward and helps people find a way to fit in and support social harmony. But in order to do so, you can't just strive too quickly for connection. You need to know, to the best of your ability, what it's like in their shoes too.

PUTTING YOURSELF IN THEIR SHOES IS KEY.

Try to understand their perspective on life without imparting your own judgment, projections, or ideas. Empathize with another in hopes of understanding their wants and needs.

Doing this is key to fundraising. It will also help you make it easier to find a connection.

---

24 Gareth Cook, "Why We Are Wired to Connect," *Scientific American*, October 22, 2013.

Growing up, my father sold herbicides for companies like Monsanto and American Cyanamid. He won awards for sales, and I remember each trophy crowding a shelf in his basement office next to old rusty farm equipment. I joke that Monsanto paid for my tap shoes. This was also my dad's first job in sales and it taught him valuable lessons he passed onto me. He had naysayers of his own. He was introducing new products every year to farmers who just wanted their crops to grow and were some of the most risk-averse potential clients out there.

His most valuable piece of advice came when I was working in Iowa. I had no idea what running a farm or living in rural America was like, let alone what farmers did in their free time.

I had over ten other campaigns trying to connect with the same caucus goers I was, and my only secret weapon was to keep showing up and doing whatever I could to find a connection with strangers. My job included making calls to the community at least four hours a night and knocking on ninety doors on Saturdays and sixty on Sundays. During the workday, I would meet with locals, organize events, enter data, and get organized for another night of calls or day of knocking doors. Knocking on doors in the summer, I'd come home covered in sweat that had dried to become salt. In the winter, I'd come home half frozen, having experienced more extreme frozen snow and ice than ever before.

One day, I finally asked my dad for advice when I was working in Iowa and couldn't figure out how to connect with some potential supporters in the more rural areas. His advice was to show up with a Snickers and a Pepsi. In the early days on the campaign, I didn't understand his advice. I wasn't doing my best to build that true connection, the connection best described by author Brené Brown as "the energy that exists between people when they feel seen, heard, and valued; when they can give and receive without judgment; and when they derive sustenance and strength from the relationship."[25]

My dad knew that one way you can make a person feel connection was through the breaking of bread: "I learned the most when a really smart farmer was shaking that Pepsi I gave him at me." My father told me this fervently over the phone as I was swamped in data entry from knocking on doors that day. "A Pepsi and a Snickers is every American male's favorite food—at least it was in the '80s and '90s. If you needed a customer to talk and get moving on buying, give 'em a Snickers. . . . The power of eating at the same time is unique in business and life. That Pepsi and Snickers may be the most unique gift they ever had the most kindness ever shown to them."

I didn't know the importance of reaching my audience on that level. This was my first job out of college. My customer service experience included a summer at Ann Taylor Loft and lifeguarding. In those first few months in Iowa, I had been asking people for support on my terms when I was most ready or had scheduled it. I hadn't thought yet to flip the scenario. When I did, it made a world of difference.

I took my dad's advice in Iowa. I would show up everywhere they were just being themselves. I went to football games

---

25 Brené Brown, LLC, "Definitions," *brenebrown.com*, accessed May 26, 2020.

with moms, ate pork sandwiches the size of my face, walked in every parade, hung out in an eighty-year-old's trailer for hours, and never turned down a glass of lemonade. I baked cookies for local Democratic meetings. I found Boy Scouts to drive their cars in small-town parades, which led to more teenagers on board. I asked about schedules and local gatherings, birthdays and report cards, and football games and town square celebrations. I found the events where people showed up and were ripe for connections.

Every minute I spent getting to know them was more important than any campaign pitch. I was making a true connection, and in the end, I won my counties. By learning what being in their shoes was like and taking my dad's advice, I was able to connect to caucus goers in ways I connect with potential donors now. Those connections drive the relationships and conversations leading donors to writing a check just like my connections helped me win delegates.

As you set off to fundraise, realize you are not just looking for donors—you're building something. The connections lead you and your prospects in the right direction. If you learn to make true connections and value the work involved, you'll build your most rewarding audience day after day.

CHAPTER 6

GETTING STARTED

Hope is the belief that our tomorrows can be better than our todays. Hope is not magic; hope is work.

—DERAY MCKESSON

Getting started is not a simple task. It's a pretty huge road-block. Anyone who says "just get started" has already faced a lot of fears, probably already knows if they are a morning lark or night owl, and has stared the beast of procrastination face-first. Getting started is never as simple as picking up a phone, a paint brush, or a baseball bat.

I want to show you that even though getting started may feel like a mountain you can't climb or don't even want to, you already have the tools you need, and the mindset you need is always within reach.

I've spent weeks on something I could have gotten done in a day. I've made excuses and proclamations for why I haven't changed bad habits, and I've had to build myself up with the best of them. The fears of asking, hearing no, and taking risks are everywhere. You can't avoid them.

It takes getting past your daydreams, intimately understanding your fantasies and procrastination, and pushing forward anyway. No secret way around it exists, but better ways through it do. So let's get started.

DON'T JUST DAYDREAM, MAKE A PLAN.

Most people don't just wake up ready to start a morning fitness regimen. Many try and fail. In the same vein, most people don't wake up ready to raise a million dollars for charity or even clean their bathroom.

But what's getting in their way?

Their fantasies, it turns out.

In comes the Wish, Outcome, Obstacle, Plan (WOOP) method because getting started is not just about thinking you can, but also understanding what's getting in the way of your start in the first place.

WOOP was created by psychologist Gabriele Oettingen. According to Oettingen, "The solution isn't to do away with dreaming and positive thinking. Rather, it's making the most of our fantasies by brushing them up against the very thing most of us are taught to ignore or diminish: the obstacles that stand in our way."[26]

The WOOP method takes you through your motivations, your daydreams, and what might get in the way, and then helps you create a plan. It's an easy framework to set yourself up before you even start, which is the challenge we're facing in the chapter anyway.

I was a night owl for a very long time and rarely worked out. I grew up playing sports but never found a fitness regimen that stuck after organized sports were no longer a thing. A few years ago, I was on a trip to California with my good friend Carolyn, and I absolutely refused to go to a 6:00 a.m. spin class with her, bemoaning the fact that someone would ever wake up that early to work out. This attitude would change, but not without a little WOOP.

I also had to admit I had some bad habits. I'm not equating starting a new fitness routine to fundraising or entrepreneurial success, but sometimes waking up before 6:00 a.m. feels like quite the accomplishment.

Beginning a fitness routine and becoming a great fundraiser aren't the same thing, but both require an essential element of behavior change: breaking bad habits. Making that first fundraising call on your list will always be the most daunting. If you have fundraising goals beyond your wildest dreams, you can't accomplish them if you have a bad habit of waiting

---

26 Anne Rautenbach, "The Downside of Positive Thinking," *New York University*, January 14, 2015.

too long to start or even follow up. You won't make that perfect pitch if you keep forgetting to spell-check or won't listen to feedback. You have to realize those bad habits and face them head on.

My coach and trainer-turned-friend Jeanie Arnold knows all of my bad habits. This is why she knows how to better help me break them and accomplish my goals. Mind you, Jeanie also used to work in fundraising at the Smithsonian. She knew about raising money for Dorothy's ruby slippers one day and the American flag the next. Knowing about fundraising and knowing my story (bad habits included) helped her better coach me. The same goes for knowing your own bad habits. Get to know them and recognize them.

It took a lot of guts to admit I had bad habits in the first place, but doing so was the key to getting started and figuring out what I needed.

According to Dr. Susan Krauss Whitbourne, "If you don't see a problem, you won't work on changing your behavior. The more honest you are with yourself about the nature of your bad habit, the more likely you will be to start on the path toward change."[27]

You should get to know your story and what's holding you back, and WOOP helps you organize these thoughts. I was going to bed too late for no real reason. I was sacrificing a lot to be there for others without prioritizing myself. I was

27 Susan Krauss Whitebourne, "5 Steps to Breaking Bad Habits," *Psychology Today*, August 23, 2011.

also in an unhealthy relationship at the time, which was emotionally abusive and just altogether taxing in hindsight. I was letting other heavy burdens be the excuses for not moving forward. I was using others' needs as a reason not to take care of myself and using TV, wine, snacks, and falling asleep on the couch on weekdays as reasons not to work out instead of reasons I needed to start. Trying to show up at six o'clock every morning with all of that going on was not easy. Not until I took the time and space to face those habits did I realize I was already on my way.

For the past five years, I've been doing Olympic-style weightlifting at 6:00 a.m. at least five to six days a week. But in learning how to show up every morning, I had to break a lot of bad habits to accomplish my goals, figure out why I had been procrastinating, and almost give up finding a fitness routine too.

But what if you are perpetually procrastinating? You're not alone; you just need to come to an understanding.

UNDERSTAND YOUR PROCRASTINATION.

Renowned author Margaret Atwood has written over fourteen novels and sixteen poetry books, and is producing even more content for Hulu's show based on her famous novel *The Handmaid's Tale*. But she is also a famous procrastinator. She embraces spending her morning worrying before entering her "writing burrow" at three in the afternoon. She's even tweeted at 10:00 p.m. about facing the "I don't know how to write" feeling. Anxiety and worrying are part of her process.[28]

Everyone procrastinates: artists, athletes, and entrepreneurs—you name it. So do fundraisers. Procrastination can be helpful to the creative process, but it can also be the largest feat to get through in order to get started. But just because it might hinder productivity doesn't mean it's all bad. Knowing how best to use your procrastination can be the key to finally getting started.

Procrastination is a beast. Understand where it's coming from and how you procrastinate and then take small steps.

Leonardo da Vinci supposedly took thirteen years to finish his famous painting *Madonna on the Rock* and sixteen years to finish the *Mona Lisa*, which was painted on top of another painting. He was also rumored to have finished *The Last Supper* because the patron threatened to cut funding.[29] You must figure out what is causing your procrastination. Leonardo da Vinci, I guess, just needed a deadline.

For you, is it timing? Are you overwhelmed by big tasks? Overwhelmed by small tasks? Easily distracted? Do you struggle with delayed gratification?[30]

---

28 Margaret E. Atwood (@MargaretAtwood), "Off to the Writing Burrow now . . . to face yet again the 'I don't know how to write' feeling . . . @ChuckWendig (It's never over)," Twitter, August 4, 2017, 10:36 p.m.

29 Sophavatey Leak, "Great Inventions from Procrastination," *UNICEF Cambodia*, September 6, 2016.

30 Jamie Ducharme, "Psychologists Explain Why You Procrastinate—And How to Stop," *TIME*, June 29, 2018.

One small thing that helps when you're in the doldrums of procrastination is to work to narrow the gap between effort and reward. Author James Surowiecki explains, "Beyond self-binding, there are other ways to avoid dragging your feet, most of which depend on what psychologists might call reframing the task in front of you. Procrastination is driven, in part, by the gap between effort (which is required now) and reward (which you reap only in the future, if ever). So narrowing that gap, by whatever means necessary, helps."[31]

Leonardo da Vinci reframed his effort within a deadline and as an opportunity to do more work. I reframed my fitness routine by reframing the reward. I just wanted a fitness routine that I enjoyed, not one that changed my life, body, or weight. It helped me clear the way to what I actually needed and quit procrastinating.

No perfect way to start exists. When I need inspiration for the gym, I watch a weightlifting competition. It reminds me how much I enjoy tinkering with the lifts and seeing what my body is capable of through strength. I was recently watching the 2019 International Weightlifting Federation World Weightlifting Championships in Pattaya, Thailand. Athlete Jolanta Wior of Poland attempted to lift 111 kilograms in clean and jerk. For a clean and jerk, you have to take the barbell off the ground and first get it to your shoulders from a squat position. Then, you must get the barbell over your head while getting into a lunge position. Wior weighed only seventy-one kilos, so she was lifting well over her body weight and had failed her first two attempts. She looked shaken and

31 James Surowiecki, "LATER," *The New Yorker*, October 4, 2010.

upset and even wiped away tears as she prepared to make her last attempt. The crowd cheered a little louder, but she still fought back tears. Then she put her hands on the bar, got in position, and made the lift with ease. Nothing about her setup was perfect. She did it anyway and succeeded. If she had not started that lift because everything wasn't in order, she never would have felt the high of getting something done when it's the last thing you want to do.

Margaret Atwood learned to comprehend and embrace her procrastination. She understands her procrastination, navigates it, and gets to work. It might not be the same for you—I would love to be able to start work at 3:00 p.m.—but seeing through the fog of procrastination and all it entails is important, because then you can truly understand how to get past it. Everyone procrastinates, but in the end, everyone has to get started.

The longer it takes you to start, the longer it takes you to finish, especially if you fall victim to bad habits, procrastination, and perfectionism. Take it from a weightlifting convert, Leonardo da Vinci, and an actual professional weightlifter, and just get started. The WOOP method can help you organize and synthesize your daydreams with your procrastination. The next step is to get started.

CHAPTER 7

TAKING A RISK

I am lucky that whatever fear I have inside me, my desire to win is always stronger.

—SERENA WILLIAMS

"It is impossible to live without failing something, unless you live so cautiously that you might as well not have lived at all, in which case you fail by default."[32] J.K. Rowling said these words in a Harvard commencement speech back in 2008. She spoke on her failures, and the biggest takeaway for me was this line about the "dangers" of being too cautious.

The thing you're afraid of, the risk, can be anything big or small that gets in your way. But your opportunity lies in how, rather than staying afraid and letting fear override your intuition, you embrace failure.

She understood the importance of risk and failure.

32 Harvard University, "J.K. Rowling Harvard Commencement Speech | Harvard University Commencement 2008," December 1, 2014, video, 21:12.

Rowling explains, "The truth is that I found success by stumbling off alone in a direction most people thought was a dead end, breaking all the 1990s shibboleths about children's books in the process," such as "male protagonists are unfashionable. Boarding schools are anathema. No kids' book should be longer than forty-five thousand words."[33]

In your career, you will often face situations in which you must act despite uncertainty. Sometimes you must act when the outcome is uncertain or lean into a gut feeling. That is especially true with the 2020 COVID-19 pandemic ravaging the globe and taking the economy down with it.

Risks come in all forms. Uncertainty is a part of life. Don't let that stop you from fundraising.

The fear of risk, of falling, of failing, of taking a chance, or of floating in the clouds of uncertainty can all be overwhelming. That fear is the image of your fingers slipping from that ledge, of falling down with nothing and no one to hold onto for safety.

Early in my career, I took a huge risk. I thought I'd lose my job. I used new technology my bosses weren't familiar with but I was—technology with very public ramifications.

Not everyone is ready to take a risk, fail, or be the sacrificial lamb. But you can be.

---

33 Kathleen Elkins, "J.K. Rowling 'Can't Stand' Following Rules—Here's What She Says to Do Instead If You Want to Succeed," *CNBC*, January 21, 2019.

SOME WILL SAY YOU'RE TAKING A RISK; OTHERS WILL REALIZE IT'S ROCK AND ROLL.

Do you think when rock and roll first came out every kid quit listening to it just because their parents told them to? Rock and roll is anything new or risky. If you want to be successful, you will have to deal with a lot of people, often in positions of power, declaring rock and roll is bad. Or they won't embrace new technology because it's too new, which is my favorite version of disparaging rock and roll.

Adopting new technology isn't always easy. And the process is not only about learning the ins and outs of how it works either. The pushback I received from my friends and parents for buying my high school prom dress online in high school in 2003 is mockable now. But then it was unheard of, risky, and out of the question.

In that same vein, I was almost fired for using technology ubiquitous with politics today.

Twitter was launched in July 2006, and my sister was an early adopter. Apple iPhones were new and Instagram didn't exist, so scrolling was limited to early Twitter adopters and blogs. I joined Twitter in 2008 and my first tweet was about a busy day of Capitol tours. I had yet to work in fundraising and was a staff assistant for my home state senator. The office was covered in Missouri memorabilia, and I had Missouri trivia cards at my desk. Around the office was a lot of beige and the sounds of printers, keyboards, and phones ringing constantly. Hierarchy reigned and everything was a power play, even to the lowest on the ladder. You knew you were a part of a bigger picture, but sometimes this was hard to see.

The US Capitol is actually one of the very few capitol buildings that is still available for a public tour even when Congress is in session. We still didn't have an online tour request system for the office, so I had a mighty binder full of not only Capitol tour requests but White House, Supreme Court, Archives, Pentagon, and so on.

One day during a break in answering the phones, I saw that Jack Dorsey, one of the founders of Twitter, was in Washington, DC, and tweeted about how beautiful the Capitol was that day. So, after a few texts to my sister, I tweeted to @Jack about whether he would be interested in a Capitol tour since I was in charge of coordinating tours for my office. I personally knew he was from St. Louis, Missouri—my hometown! I never ever thought he would respond to my tweet.

But he did. The founder of Twitter replied to my tweet. He wanted a tour!

I messaged my sister. I called my mom. They were both over the moon. I squealed with delight and almost scared a constituent on the phone before I was able to come to my senses. This was something big, and I felt like I'd landed the lead in a play and was about to start the opening act.

As soon as @Jack replied to my tweet, I immediately went to tell our recently hired new media staffer, who was elated. He listened to how I followed @Jack on Twitter and how I simply saw he was in DC. I couldn't wait to give Jack a tour. We couldn't wait to tell senior staff about it. He coached me on how to pitch it, how to present it, but couldn't see any negatives. Most of the conversation happened in the hallway;

it felt like we had this magical secret to share and had somehow pulled off a stunt.

The new media staffer and I got to the office and explained the fantastic news with enormous smiles. Our smiles, however, faded as soon as we saw the reaction on the senior staffer's face. Her brow sharpened into a dagger and her lower jaw began to work, as if she were grinding the words that were about to come out of her mouth. Her words were simple but effective.

"Meredith, NO."

But turning back now was not an option.

What I thought was initiative and as easy to enjoy as rock and roll was overshadowed by entrenched behaviors of establishment and many decisions out of my control. I was afraid I'd lose my job. I was told to delete the tweets—I had made a grave mistake. I knew if this was how I lost my job in the Senate, at least I'd have a good story. I didn't know what would happen next.

Despite this uncertainty, Jack got a great tour and I got to give it to him. We visited the room where senators once debated slavery, which was the same room senators debated President Clinton's impeachment. We walked under the Capitol dome and swirled around to take in the entire frieze depicting American history with George Washington surrounded by thirteen angels representing the original thirteen colonies. I pointed out staffers bustling through corridors and hidden statues of established politicians of yore, and brought him back to our office for a meeting with the senator.

He got to meet his home state senator and talk about his innovations and local St. Louis delicacies before he headed to the White House for the rest of the day. The meeting made the news, I didn't get fired, and my office never spoke of it again.

However, I had been in the middle of a debate about new technology and how to embrace it. I'd forced their hand at taking a risk and felt the pressure of someone in power wielding it to make me feel small. But I don't regret it, and I'm still friends with that new media staffer.

I would keep this story close to the chest for a long time because I was still worried it would backfire. But over a decade has passed, and I think the story has aged well.

BEING THE SACRIFICIAL LAMB IS OKAY.

Not every risk has to end in your own success. It still matters, regardless.

Howard Dean's campaign turned campaign organizing on its head. Barack Obama would take the lessons learned by the Dean campaign and break records.

But most people know the Dean campaign for slowly crumbling after he let out a loud scream the night he lost the Iowa caucus. But he was revolutionary when it came to using technology and online fundraising. As a young campaign intern in New Hampshire in 2004, I didn't realize what I was seeing play out in front of me or the importance of the Howard Dean campaign as a sacrificial lamb.

The first campaign I ever interned on was the Wes Clark presidential primary campaign in the winter of 2004. Clark skipped the Iowa caucus because he entered the race too late and headed straight to New Hampshire. That internship was how I witnessed the Dean campaign up close.

They harnessed technology to organize a movement and started a revolution in fundraising. His campaign manager Joe Trippi explains, "No mainstream presidential candidate had ever made his fundraising goals transparent for the world to see. Which was all the more reason we needed to do it."[34] They published their fundraising goals in fundraising emails, focused on small-dollar donations, and used online organizing as much as they could before Facebook and other online portals existed. They put all of their momentum on the line to try something new in a world with pretty strict rules for the road.

In being the first campaign to embrace the Internet and use online organizing, the Howard Dean campaign paved the way for the Barack Obama campaign in 2008. Dean's campaign toppled any previous record easily and raised millions from over hundreds of thousands of donors.[35]

---

34 Joe Trippi, *The Revolution Will Not Be Televised* (New York, NY: Regan, 2004), 130.

35 Bill Scher, "4 ways Howard Dean changed American Politics," *The Week*, June 21, 2013.

But he lost.

What if Dean hadn't embraced technology and created a movement?

His campaign paved the way for others further down the line.

President Barack Obama would go on to break Dean's fund-raising records, lean heavily on online fundraising, and also turn down public financing, just like Dean.

Sometimes it takes a sacrificial lamb to launch something even brighter into the future. Don't diminish the risks you take because you could just be paving the way, completely unbeknownst to you.

You must push forward. You must know the risks are out there—but you'll survive. You must be patient as those around you question every step.

Howard Dean took campaign finance and technology and turned them on their head. He changed politics forever. To write *Harry Potter*, J.K. Rowling went against the established rules for success in children's books. I used Twitter on Capitol Hill. Taking the risk is worth it.

CHAPTER 8

GOALS

Our goals can only be reached through a vehicle of a plan, in which we must fervently believe, and upon which we must vigorously act. There is no other route to success.

—PABLO PICASSO

Oprah Winfrey sets high goals, Richard Branson says to write them down, and Tony Robbins calls goals dreams with a deadline. Everyone has a different way around it, but they all set goals.[36]

Goals aren't something to be afraid of, but they can often be an intimidating part of the process.

Goals will always be a big part of any fundraiser's success. I was so excited about the first job I got in DC, working on Capitol Hill. But every day felt like I was just pushing the same boulder up the actual hill of Capitol Hill. I missed the

36 "HOW TO SET GOALS ACCORDING TO 3 SUCCESSFUL ENTREPRENEURS," Boss In Heels, accessed May 26, 2020.

finite time associated with goals and how I knew whether I'd accomplished my goal or not by the numbers. Goals to me were predictions of success—a bet on your performance, a premonition of your achievement. Goals were a vital part of accomplishing what I would set out to do. Then I finally got into fundraising.

I remember the tiny fundraising office where I got my start. Looking at an empty calendar knowing I had to fill each weekday with a breakfast, lunch, and reception and for each event we were raising at least fifteen to thirty thousand dollars. I remember overhearing bosses discuss how our clients hadn't started fundraising soon enough and were now a long shot if we didn't raise millions and set those goals ahead of us. I struggled but also accomplished huge goals there. We had white board calendars all over the office that were almost grey from filing in and erasing events for the next month's goals. Somehow, we always beat our goals. It helped me understand the importance of making goals, but at the time it just felt good beating them.

You might find yourself with a goal to raise one thousand dollars or even ten million dollars for any kind of cause. Whether you're a novice or a savant, breaking down and understanding your goals is a great first step. Beyoncé has had plenty of goals.

Beyoncé's first career goal was to raise enough money singing at her mother's hair salon so she could afford a pass to

Six Flags.[37] Beyoncé would take this goal-setting habit with her throughout her life, eventually becoming the first African American woman to headline Coachella and the third woman to headline the Super Bowl. This is the power of setting goals.

GOALS FEEL GOOD.

Whether you like it or not, having a goal is better than nothing at all.

After just one year of running my first political action committee (PAC) at UBS, my boss, who is still a mentor of mine, left the company. He'd set big goals for us, and we'd achieved them. Andy Blocker showed me how to focus, how to calm down, and how to go after it. He also showed me what it meant to be a good mentor.

My first year there, we set out to increase the receipts of the PAC every single quarter, indefinitely. My longest tenure anywhere had been two years, so I felt like this was just another election cycle. I would end up staying for five years. We would search out events where we could raise money and groups we could reach out to, and we would always be finding a way to increase the receipts coming in. He kept moving the goalpost, and my confidence grew. He was setting me up for success.

---

37 Malia Robinson, "What Beyoncé Has Accomplished In 32 Years Is Mind-Blowing," *Business Insider*, September 4, 2013.

But even when I was feeling like a million bucks after landing donor after donor, he made sure to explain the goals for each event. He explained the reason why I could go after them and when. He showed me all the work put into getting the operations in place so I could do just that. He told me the story of why they hired me specifically. We looked at the smaller goals and made sure we had a good system for follow-up. We looked at my personal career growth. We looked at how I handled the different leadership and how to slow down my pitch. I got better and better and soon felt like a well-oiled machine that could never stop raising money. It felt good.

According to Madhuleena Roy Chowdhury, "Goals play a dominant role in shaping the way we see ourselves and others. A person who is focused and goal-oriented is likely to have a more positive approach towards life and perceive failures as temporary setbacks, rather than personal shortcomings.[38]

After Andy left UBS, I kept fundraising and those goals helped pave the way. That next year, with him gone, I spent most of my time trying to keep our Democratic relationships healthy on the Hill and just running the PAC in survival mode. That was until a few years later when I read the Christmas card from the PAC board director. Inside it had the regular typed basic holiday greeting and winter scene photo, but he had also written, "You are the growth engine." I smiled from ear to ear. I was setting and beating my own goals.

---

38 Madhuleena Roy Chowdhury, "The Science & Psychology of Goal-Setting 101," *Positive Psychology*, December 2, 2020.

When Andy left, he'd been adamant that it was a good thing. He told me his leaving would show how I could fundraise on my own, but I didn't believe him until I saw that Christmas card. If I can do anything, I want to remind you that YOU are the growth engine. You can set your goals. You can keep learning. You can fundraise on your own. So channel your inner Beyoncé and set some goals.

SET GOOD GOALS.

Beyoncé never just showed up; she puts in the work and understands the value of different types of goals. Andy Blocker knew the importance of setting goals every step of the way and goals around more than just results.

Both Beyoncé and Andy understand the three main types of goals: Process, Performance and Outcome.

Positivepsychology.com today defines them:[39]

- The Process Goals **(Behaviors)**: Process goals (also called procedural goals) are the **behaviors** or the strategies that will help us to perform well and increase our chances of achieving our desired outcome goals.
- The Performance Goals **(Standards)**: Performance goals set the **standards** at which we will perform our process goals.
- The Outcome Goals **(Results)**: Outcome goals are specific and spell out the **results** you hope to achieve in the end.

---

39 Ibid.

When Andy left and I was alone fundraising for the PAC, I was lost at first. Then I remembered all the different types of goals we set together. I knew I didn't just have to focus on the results but could also set goals for standards and behaviors.

In each of these types of goals, you can find ways to better understand where to refine your own fundraising goals. Maybe you've been focused solely on the outcome and are missing out on ways to work on the process and performance, both of which help your outcome tremendously. Or maybe you have the best process in place but are struggling with the performance, so you've yet to hit the outcome. I've fallen into this trap by focusing more on having the most beautiful call sheet instead of realizing my ask was all wrong or even getting to the ask at all.

Then came the next few years and a new job. I made time to set goals. Maybe it's because of business school, but process goals are my favorite of recent. I think this is because once you get a good system in place, a solid process you can use, then it makes all the other types of goals easier.

When I first started a new job in fundraising, I missed a huge opportunity. I'd completely forgotten to set any goals. In fundraising, your goals can't just be about the money coming in the door. You'll miss out on really achieving success and won't set yourself up for later either.

I was very clear over the next few years about my goals, even to the chagrin of executives. I've told heads of finance stagnant receipts were good and told CEOs I was really proud of how much equity we were sweating—the corporate euphemism for potentially spending more than you'd normally want to in order to see the results you want.

But watching a Netflix special, I saw all of these goals at work in tandem.

I was watching the Netflix special Cheer when a quote from the head coach of Navarro Cheerleading rang out loud. Head Coach Monica was describing their practice ethic and explained, "You keep going until you get it right, and then you keep going until you can't get it wrong."[40] They work on their process goals the hardest to make the rest of the goals easier too. They had their final performance in mind (outcome), they committed to doing forty-one "full-outs," or full routines, before competition day (performance).

If they had only focused on one type of goal, I don't think they would be champions over ten times and counting.

Candidates for office are often laser-focused on goals, as is their fundraising staff.

Every candidate fundraiser has goals for raising money. A fundraiser makes quarterly and yearly goals. Some fundraisers earn more based on if their candidate wins, and some earn more based on total money raised. Every fundraiser is essentially raising their salary. So once you've got an idea of your goal in mind and have recognized the different types involved, now is the time to get to setting your goals. The

---

40 *Cheer,* season 1, episode 3, "Blood, Sweat, and Tears," directed by Greg Whitley, aired January 8, 2020, on Netflix.

best way to do that is to make SMART goals. Setting SMART goals can make it a whole lot easier.

George Doran introduced the acronym SMART goals in 1981, which stands for:

- **Specific** (simple, sensible, and significant)
- **Measurable** (meaningful and motivating)
- **Achievable** (agreed and attainable)
- **Relevant** (reasonable, realistic and resourced, and results-based)
- **Time-Bound** (time-based, time-limited, time-/cost-limited, timely, and time-sensitive)[41]

With the way the current system is set up, if you want to run for office, you have to raise a lot of money. The process is painful and tedious, and it doesn't stop once you've won. You are putting yourself out on the line, hearing no, and spending hours practically locked in a closet. I know, because I've been there. Senator Kay Hagan (D-NC) was one of my favorite candidates to raise money for and with early in my career.

Did you know fundraising can take up to 50 percent of an elected member of Congress's day?[42] This is one of the reasons I think we need to take a long, hard look at how the system is set up, but let's stay focused on goals for now.

41 "The History and Evolution of SMART Goals," *AchieveIt*, accessed May 26, 2020.

42 Gabby Weiss, "GUIDE: The Basics of Fundraising for a Political Campaign," *NGPVAN*, September 10, 2018.

Here's what we knew: Senator Hagan was a candidate who was running for a **specific** office, she needed a **measurable** amount of money to get there, she knew that winning is **achievable**, and she feel public service was **relevant**. Lastly, we all knew the days left until election day, so we were very **time bound**.

A good senator could say their entire smart goal in one sentence:

"Hello, this is Senator So-and-So. I am running for Senate in my state and I need this much money to support my campaign, which is an important campaign, and we have a quarterly deadline/the election is soon."

I would hope they would be more eloquent than that, but it makes the point.

The current process of candidate fundraising and call time is so tedious that the finance assistants have to protect call time from being used for other purposes on a campaign, and once a member of Congress is elected, scheduling that time is even harder. I would bring favorite snacks and even barter with more fun calls to famous people just to keep call time going. Senator Kay Hagan of North Carolina was an incredible fundraiser who never missed her call time, but it took a lot of trail mix and iced tea. But every time we went in that call time room, we knew we were part of a SMART goal.

CHAPTER 9

SELF-AWARENESS

Take criticism seriously, not personally. If there is truth or merit in the criticism, try to learn from it. Otherwise, let it roll right off you.

—HILLARY CLINTON

I've been told no every week I've gone into the office.
I've been told I should be ashamed of what I do.
I've been told I was too aggressive and then too timid.
I've been told I needed to take it slow only to succeed going fast.
I've failed and then survived every time.

It took mistakes and failures personally until I learned—and relearned—a valuable lesson: This is not about you. This is not even about being right. This is about understanding and providing a space to be seen and heard. This is about being able to take criticism in stride and truly embracing what's at play and very much outside of your control.

Let's make one thing very clear. In fundraising, the goals, results, and even failures are never going to be 100 percent about you. You might be the one raising the money, the one stressing out, the one putting yourself on the line, the one making the connection to the donor, and the one stressing about the big ask. But in reality, the less you take the process and results personally and the more you know your fundraising numbers are about so much else, the easier this entire thing will be.

Even if you struggle with self-awareness, at the very least take a crack at understanding it's not about you.

My top three ways to knowing it's not about you:

1. Grow a thick skin.
2. Don't blame yourself—instead listen harder.
3. Fail your own way.

GROW A THICK SKIN.

Fundraising isn't all offense. The defense is your thick skin and ability to let naysayers and nos just slide right off of you. Sadly, the first step to growing the thick skin you need is to realize you need it. As with many other parts of fundraising, just getting started is half the battle.

I grew some of my thickest skin just two months into a new job. It was an exciting new role and one I'd worked hard to achieve. I'd be working with some elite people in the government relations field, and they needed my help. They'd warned me it was going to be challenging, but I felt I was ready. I'd worked in the industry, so I wasn't afraid. After about two months, I gave the go-ahead on a mass fundraising email to over seventy thousand employees while in the middle of attending a huge department gathering out of town, and I didn't think twice.

I'd been in fundraising for almost ten years at that point, and had only experienced inquiries here and there with some people ghosting or saying no. I didn't know it, but I wasn't ready for what I got back from that email, less than a quarter in at my new job.

I received ample angry responses. People responded asking things like, why did my job function exist and how dare I raise money from them? A few said they were disgusted with my ask, they never wanted to hear from me again, and were even offended by the ask. I immediately took it personally and assumed it was my fault. I cried. I'd been in fundraising for years, but I assumed it was something I'd said, how I said it, or that I missed something critical since I was so new to the company.

There I was sitting in a meeting trying not to cry. I was surrounded by big windows and corporate slogans. Busy type As were ready to network their way to success and all I wanted to do was wallow. I kept rereading the emails while sitting alone in my cramped hotel room and getting more and more upset. I didn't know what to do or what lesson to learn. I had to get ready for the reception that night at some fancy space in Chicago, and all I wanted to do was curl up and blame myself.

I tried to hold it in, but my new coworkers saw me crying later that night. It took three strong women and a strong-willed boss to turn my frown upside down. I looked to them for answers, but they didn't have any. They didn't place blame. They didn't feel sorry for me. Instead, they told me stories of how they too had to grow thicker skin. They patted me on the back and wrote off every insult. They grabbed me a glass of champagne and declared the behavior in those responses below the belt. They were my hype girls and reassurance because they had been there too. My bosses were more concerned about me than any of the naysayers. They knew those responses had nothing to do with me. They sat me down and handed me a big dose of reality: I needed to grow a thicker skin. Everyone has to grow their own thick skin. It took a lesson ten years in the industry to finally grow that thick skin I needed.

DON'T BLAME YOURSELF.

When my coworkers were comforting me, they never said what happened was my fault. They never said I'd failed, and they never ridiculed my efforts. I worked hard that next year to grow tougher skin, but I still had to work on not blaming myself. Then I learned a trick that works every time: listening.

It frees up time and mental processing to realize you can keep moving forward without having to take it personally. But it's tough. Believe me.

According to Michael J. Formica, MS, MA, EdM, "Self-blame is one of the most toxic forms of emotional abuse. It amplifies our perceived inadequacies, whether real or imagined, and paralyzes us before we can even begin to move forward."[43] Don't get trapped in self-blame! This is one of the hardest pieces of advice I have to follow.

I remember once when I was swirling in self-blame from a tough day at work, a tough week with other drama, and just all in all being pretty hard on myself. My skin was getting hot, my fists were clenched, and my jaw was tight. I screamed through tears, "I'm so mad I'm so hard on myself!" within five minutes of getting home from work.

My husband started laughing. I looked at him, befuddled. He was an incredible listener and I needed him in that moment. I wanted him to say, "YEAH! I agree!" But instead, he calmly and kindly said to me, "You were just hard on yourself about being hard on yourself. Did you hear that?"

I wanted to scream, but I started to laugh. I hadn't been listening even to myself. I was paralyzing myself instead of listening. Thankfully he was.

We can't always have a loved one there to help us when we're swirling in self-blame, but when you get a quick no in fundraising, jumping right on the self-blame ship is easy. The easiest way to avoid ever getting on board is getting better at listening. Your skin will grow thick as needed the longer you fundraise, but to protect yourself from a calloused sense of self is to focus on listening instead.

---

43 Michael Formica, "Self-Blame: The Ultimate Emotional Abuse," *Psychology Today*, April 19, 2013.

People just want to be heard. Listening will help you understand this is not about you. You'll get better at conversations and better at identifying with your potential donor. SoulCycle founder Julie Rice values listening in all of her employees so much so that she teaches it. "Teaching people how to listen and to have conversations is something that is so important," Rice said, "I think that training people how to—to listen to what somebody else has to say, allows people who then have issues to go and be heard."[44]

Sometimes I frame the act of the ask as an effort to figure out what I need to listen to the potential donor about. I will find what topic they want to share and what they care about, and that will help me make my ask down the line. This helps change the topic to something that keeps my prospect in a better mood and then they are in a better mental space to hear what I have to say or ask.

Don't you want the key to the personality of your top donor? Your potential investor? As I continue to fundraise from employees, I have found feeling heard is crucial for employees because it is vital to understanding your potential donors.

In listening more attentively and purposely, don't forget you'll find the secret trick to not taking things personally too. It might take setting personal politics to the side, but at the end of the day, control what you can control, especially self-blame.

---

44 Tim Ferris and Julie Rice, "#372: Julie Rice — Co-Founding SoulCycle, Taming Anxiety, and Mastering Difficult Conversations," June 5, 2019, in *The Tim Ferris Show*, produced by Tim Ferris, podcast, MP3 audio, 43:48.

FAIL YOUR OWN WAY.

You may know how to listen, grow thick skin, and not blame yourself. But have you ever thought about how you fail? One of the last steps to truly knowing this is not about you is understanding the best way to fail is to fail your own way.

Amy Poehler is one of my favorite actresses and entrepreneurs. She has a thing or two to say about failure. She's also grown a thick skin from improv comedy, *Saturday Night Live*, Hollywood, and maneuvering a male-dominated field. She's not shy to talk about it: "I've failed a million times on stage, just not getting laughs. I've listened to notes that I knew weren't right. I've pitched ideas and let other people change them, knowing that it was the wrong choice. The question you have to ask yourself is: How do you want to fail? Do you want to fail in a way that feels like it respects your tastes and value system?"[45]

When I produced that massive email and cried my way through the responses, I was not prepared for what would come. No one is prepared to fail. But you can know that if you fail, you've done it your own way. The failure and angry messages felt worse because I'd taken notes from consultants and too many senior leaders and had just pushed to get the solicitation email out the door. I hadn't sat down and looked at what I really wanted to achieve, what needed to be done to succeed, and how I wanted to do it. Instead I was flailing around in my own negative feelings and hadn't realized it.

---

45 Christopher Rosa and Samantha Leach, "12 Famous Women on Facing—and Overcoming—Failure," *Glamour*, January 29, 2019.

I had to learn how to make the failures on my own while not blaming myself. Once I did that, my mindset shifted, and I felt ready for the solicitation the next year.

Free yourself from that burden, those feelings that keep taking up too much space in your brain and making loud noises like someone emptying the dishwasher too early in the morning. Taking things too seriously can be ruinous for a fundraiser. Let what's out of your control stay outside, value your failures with grace and laughter, get to know yourself better, and then, grow a thick skin.

CHAPTER 10

WHERE DO WE GO FROM HERE?

Who cares if Gryzzl and Ron have more money? I have the most valuable currency in America. A blind stubborn belief that what I am doing is 100 percent right.

—LESLIE KNOPE, *PARKS AND RECREATION*

I love that quote. It reminds me of the attitude you should have when you're fundraising. Do you feel that way yet? I believe everyone has the power and skills to get started as a fundraiser. You just might not feel ready to use that power or those skills.

Struggle will occur. But have you ever heard anyone say, "I wish I worried more," or "I wish I'd stressed out more"? No. Because none of that helps you in the long run.

You will be tested and you will be scared, but you've also learned this is all part of the game of being a fundraiser.

YOU WILL BE TESTED.

I increased the receipts at my first PAC job by 30 percent in my first year. I thought I knew exactly how to fundraise at every PAC and that I could replicate my performance as soon as I walked in the door at my new job. I was wrong. But I did not see it as a failure. I saw it as a test. I guess I just didn't know I needed it.

Jeni Britton Bauer, entrepreneur and founder of Jeni's Ice Cream, dropped out of college to start her business. But did you know her business almost failed because of a listeria scare? She has been tested multiple times and has now embraced it, explaining, "Every year you get tested and you get stronger. You build more resilience. It becomes who you are." She has grown a twenty-five-million-dollar business that employs 550 employees with 1,700 retail locations.[46]

But did you know she was almost shut down by regulators? After returning to the same market in Ohio she'd started her first ice cream business with a new small business loan and a new name, regulators came to tell her she was operating without a milk processing license and would have to open a separate kitchen. After having to open up a separate location and betting on scaling, Jeni's Ice Cream was able to build the successful business.

---

46 Kimberly Weisel, "Only Crazy Obsession Could Have Built This $25 Million Ice Cream Empire," *Inc.*, December 4, 2014.

She isn't just building a business, but building employees—or, as Jeni likes to call them, "Ice Cream Jedis"—who have survived tests and can learn from them.[47]

When I struggled to replicate my performance of PAC fundraising, I was not acting like someone who had been tested and learned from it. I needed to look for what I was missing. What else was involved? What could be the cause outside of my control? I came in with a lot of assumptions and my confidence was shot, but I took a step back and realized I'd had passed my first test at my new job. Then the next year, I cut cancellations in half and increased the average gift per new donor by over one hundred dollars.

Nathaniel Lambert, PhD, explains, "Growing because of trials can be compared to the oyster that has a little piece of sand lodged inside. In response to this intruder, the oyster makes the most of its trial and makes a beautiful pearl! Without the challenge or setback of having this uncomfortable piece of sand, the oyster would never have made the pearl."[48]

I never would have been able to figure out how to decrease cancellations and increase the average per donor if I hadn't been all but knocked out on my first go-around. I'm glad I was tested.

---

47 Kimberly Weisel, "Only Crazy Obsession Could Have Built This $25 Million Ice Cream Empire," *Inc.*, December 4, 2014.

48 Nathaniel Lambert, "How Greater Challenges Help You Grow," *Psychology Today,* August 22, 2014.

BEING A LONG SHOT IS OKAY.

My first job out of college was my hardest job to date. It was also for a losing campaign. I learned how to drive in snow and sleet and would listen to a Beyoncé and Alicia Keys album on repeat. I scared multiple cows when I'd open up the door during rural canvassing trying to figure out what wrong turn I'd taken, since this was before most people had iPhones and I didn't have a GPS.

Even though I worked on a losing campaign, I still did good work. I still learned valuable lessons and put myself out there. Remember Howard Dean's campaign? He didn't win, but they taught future campaigns how to use the web to their advantage. Imagine if they hadn't tried. He was a long shot.

Sometimes being the long shot is good. Long shot bias is when people overvalue long shots and undervalue favorites. Why not take advantage and help your cause? Why not use that to your advantage?

Long shots who take a chance help move things forward, and that's something to be proud of. Sometimes your long shot just might pay off. My favorite long shot story is Senator Chris Coons of Delaware. He ran for Senate the first time in 2010. I graduated from University of Delaware in 2007 and interned on the Jack Markell for Treasurer campaign while I was a student. I remember Coons was the New Castle county executive at the time.

While at UD, I took as many classes on campaigns as I could. Classes and undergraduate lifestyle aside, one of my favorite memories was attending the Delaware Return Day

Celebration. In Delaware, they literally bury a hatchet. Everyone from both parties attends, and candidates have to ride in a carriage with their opponent. That year, 2006, Christine O'Donnell, a conservative Republican activist, was among the candidates. I was in my preppy phase, and I remember her commenting how she liked the pearls I was wearing with my campaign t-shirt. Years later, in 2010, the public would meet O'Donnell when she beat incumbent Delaware Senator Mike Castle in the Republican primary.

She beat a mammoth in the political world of Delaware and would be running against Chris Coons who, up until that moment, had been a sacrificial lamb and a huge long shot. They practically take turns in Delaware, so an upset like O'Donnell was huge. She then went on to air a now infamous commercial where she explained, "I am not a witch," and lost the general election. But the lesson I glean is that it took two long shots to elect Chris Coons. One was O'Donnell throwing her hat in the primary and the other was Coons putting his name on the ballot, even if beating then-Representative Mike Castle was a long shot. Both O'Donnell and Coons fundraised to be those long shots, to show up, and in the end, it was a long shot who won.

It goes to show you never know just how close you are to winning, so you should never stop fundraising.

Jeni's Ice Cream is still a success today, and Chris Coons is still a senator. The tests make you stronger, and when you're a long shot, the success is that much sweeter—almost as sweet as Jeni's Ice Cream.

CHAPTER 11

YOU ARE A FUNDRAISER

Every year you get tested and you get stronger. You build more resilience. It becomes who you are.

—JENI BRITTON BAUER

I'm a fundraiser. Are you?

As you've read through this book, you've hopefully been able to identify with some of the fears, roadblocks, and stories along my path to becoming and succeeding as a fundraiser: a path filled with ups and downs and plenty of twists and turns.

As you get started on your fundraising journey, I want to simplify the lessons into three traits I believe epitomize every fundraiser.

Fundraisers are resilient. Fundraisers have a sense of efficacy. Fundraisers are also very self-aware.

RESILIENCE

Resilience is a firm acceptance of reality, strong values about life's meaning, and a rather bizarre ability to invent or improvise.[49] It's not optimism, and it's not just the ability to trudge through roadblocks. Resilient people face their fears.

J.K. Rowling, whom we talked about before and who I wish would change her stance on transgender people, is famous for writing the *Harry Potter* series and is also a great example of resilience at work. She was contemplating suicide, living on state benefits, and working out of cafes in Edinburgh, Scotland. Her first manuscript for *Harry Potter* was turned down by twelve different publishers.

Did you know her first green light is said to have happened because the daughter of the publisher had read her first chapter and demanded another? It took a year from being turned down by twelve publishers before an eight-year-old got her hands on it. That eight-year-old happened to be the daughter of a very important publisher. But what if Rowling had given up trying, if she hadn't invented, improvised, and accepted her reality and stayed strong?

The military actually teaches resiliency, which is "designed to help people cope with adversity, adapt to change, and overcome challenges.[50] If *Harry Potter* exists because of resilience and the military has its own training program, I hope you're convinced resilience is a great trait to have.

---

49 Charone Houri, "A Hidden and Forgotten Story about Resilience," *Medium*, August 2, 2018.

50 "Military Resiliency Training," *Good Therapy*, accessed on May 26, 2020.

EFFICACY

I think efficacy is the most important trait in a fundraiser.

Efficacy in pharmacology describes the maximum response that can be achieved with a drug, while efficacy in elections is described as "one's individual sense of how effective one's vote will be in influencing the political process."[51], [52]

Efficacy is not confidence. Efficacy is the belief in your ability and your role in affecting the goal or change at hand. So much of efficacy is feeling the need and understanding the power in showing up.

Fundraisers have to find an audience and make the ask to keep raising money. Athletes have to start the game, make the shot, and run the race. Artists have to start from a blank canvas, and authors have to start somewhere too. Each person needs the feeling of efficacy, or else they would never show up in the first place.

Right now, we're facing record low voter participation and record low political efficacy. Voters do not feel like their efforts matter in the end and more people don't vote than do, even in the general elections. [53]

---

51 "POLITICAL EFFICACY AND VOTER TURNOUT," *Bill of Rights Institute*, accessed on May 26, 2020.

52 Ananya Mandal, "What Does Efficacy Mean?" *News Medical Life Sciences*, June 20, 2019.

53 Christopher Ingraham, "Low voter turnout is no accident, according to a ranking of the ease of voting in all 50 states," Washington Post, October 22, 2018.

Voters feel like the decision has been made before they even show up to vote. I blame some of this on over suppression. But even so, more and more states vote in the presidential primary election on Super Tuesday in early March because they want to feel like they matter. Self-efficacy is about feeling like what you do matters.

According to psychologist Albert Bandura, a person's attitudes, abilities, and cognitive skills comprise what is known as the self-system. This system plays a major role in how we perceive situations and how we behave in response to different situations. Self-efficacy is an essential part of this self-system:

- People with a strong sense of self-efficacy:
  - View challenging problems as tasks to be mastered
  - Develop a deeper interest in the activities in which they participate
  - Form a stronger sense of commitment to their interests and activities
  - Recover quickly from setbacks and disappointments

- People with a weak sense of self-efficacy:
  - Avoid challenging tasks
  - Believe difficult tasks and situations are beyond their capabilities
  - Focus on personal failings and negative outcomes
  - Quickly lose confidence in personal abilities[54]

54 Kendra Cherry, "Self Efficacy and Why Believing in Yourself Matters," *VeryWell Mind*, May 17, 2020.

If you look at the weak self-efficacy points, you'll find a lot of the fears we have faced in this book.

All of your fears won't disappear, but I know no matter what type of fundraising I do and for how long I do it, I'll be able to affect the goal at hand. Maybe I believe I'm right or just that I can help as we figure it out along the way.

SELF-AWARENESS

Self-awareness has been described as "all about knowing your emotions, your personal strengths and weaknesses, and having a strong sense of your own worth."[55]

Looking back, I realize I got a heavy dose of awareness lessons after the John Edwards campaign folded in 2008.

My candidate lost. My first job just dissolved. I thought he was my road to the White House. Then it turned out he was cheating on his wife who had cancer too. I was twenty-three and had just started working in politics. I could have just stopped there. I sure thought about it. But the campaign and its blunders were not about me. I gave it another try, went with another, and I'm still in politics today. I had early career lessons in self-awareness, you probably did too. Have you ever actually been okay with a plan B? That's self-awareness at work.

Instead of seeing the start of my career a loss, I look back on the lessons I learned earlier than most, the incredible

55 "Self-Awareness," Skills You Need, accessed May 26, 2020.

experience of being in the middle of it all, and the relationships I made with kind, hardworking people in Iowa. I recently asked Debby Kurry, one of my precinct captains in Iowa, about our time working together. She didn't mention how the campaign lost, she didn't focus on all that hard work, but instead talked about an event we pulled together near the end of the campaign and our relationship and good times together.

Fundraisers can't focus on only the receipts and can't focus on only the goals. They see the bigger picture and are aware of the individual role they play in the grand scheme. In that awareness, they find strength to keep going against all odds to raise money.

You are a fundraiser no matter how many times you're tested, how much of a long shot you are when you start, or if you candidate loses too.

CHAPTER 12

CONCLUSION

Whenever you find yourself on the side of the majority, it is time to pause and reflect.

—MARK TWAIN

Take a pause.

Give yourself a second to think about how you want to use the lessons of this book.

Can you use them to help you raise funds? Ask for what you want? Cope with the tribulations of a worldwide pandemic? Stand up for what's right and join movements for justice?

Think about the lessons and stories about working through your fear of no, identify any insecurities about whether you feel you have what it takes to be a fundraiser, or reflect a bit in the lessons around self-awareness and risk.

Really, take a pause.

Life is navigated in the pauses. Navigating big decisions during all of the exciting, difficult, happy, or sad moments—or even in all the glorious peaks and tremendous valleys—can be hard. That's why feeling your feelings is important. Be as present as you can, and do your best.

I wrote most of this book in 2019, before any of us knew about the coronavirus or yet another violent act prompting public outrage and a civil rights revolution. Like so many of you, I'm currently in a huge pause as the world confronts the COVID-19 pandemic. Our world is changing right now, and we don't know what it will look like in the months and years to come. But we can focus on the good that is happening all around us every day. This collective pause has allowed for new creativity, deeper introspection, and new ways to accept the unknown and the uncomfortableness that comes with that.

A million factors are at play at any given time in our history. Making decisions is different now too. Many of us wish we had more data, especially in this seemingly never-ending roller coaster of a pause we find ourselves in. To better understand how to make decisions and create a path forward, I keep coming back to terms I heard over and over in business school: understanding your risk tolerance and risk capacity.

RISK TOLERANCE AND RISK CAPACITY

Risk tolerance is defined as "the amount of risk that an investor is comfortable taking or the degree of uncertainty that an investor is able to handle," while risk capacity is defined as "the amount of risk that the investor 'must' take in order to reach their financial goals."[56]

For an investor, the tolerance is about what kinds of financial risk they are willing to take in order to see the returns they want to see in the time they want to see it. As a fundraiser, I equate it to how risky following up with a donor is when I've already contacted about a contribution.

Is it worth asking again if they might think I'm bothering them? What's at stake? A huge check? A small check? The answers to those questions help me decide just how much risk I'm willing to take before I make that call. Risk capacity is even simpler. A risk you HAVE to take as a fundraiser is calling someone, asking for money, and them laughing in your face. If you need to spend money, you have to raise money. What is the amount of risk you have the capacity to take versus the degree to which you feel comfortable?

In his article "Fundraising as Risk Assessment and Management" for the Association of Fundraising Professionals, Cherian Koshy discusses the top three things that fundraising professionals "need to consider immediately to reverse this course of action that will imperil our missions, undermine our programs, and doom us to irrelevance":

56 Barclay Palmer, "What Is the Difference Between Risk Tolerance and Risk Capacity?" *Investopedia*, February 27, 2020.

1. Stop approaching risk haphazardly.
2. Stop conflating causation and correlation
3. Think! (understanding what your data reveals and hides)[57]

To summarize, Koshy wants fundraising professionals to understand risk well enough that they see its role in what they do every day.

Looking ahead at any fundraising, from startups to nonprofits to, of course, politics, you'll be faced with making decisions about who and how to interact with the public and your donor base. You'll be faced with making decisions about when and how to start a fundraising campaign, even if everyone is still struggling through a pandemic, healing from generational trauma, or recovering from another political election. You'll also see that sometimes inaction speaks louder than action. Understanding how much risk you and your organization are able to tolerate will help you make those tough choices about what your role could be in order to help build a positive reputation and help affect meaningful change.

I hope I have inspired the fundraiser inside of you and that the lessons in this book have helped you pick up the phone and make an ask. I hope I've provided you with some stories and skills to build upon as you raise funds for those who need your help.

Take the pause, take the risk, and know that **you are a fundraiser**.

---

57 Cherian Koshy, "Fundraising as Risk Assessment and Management," *Association of Fundraising Professionals*, August 8, 2019.

APPENDIX

INTRODUCTION

Clark, Kate. "Venture capital investment in US companies to hit $100B in 2018." *Tech Crunch*, October 9, 2018. *https://techcrunch.com/2018/10/09/venture-capital-investment-in-us-companies-to-hit-100b-in-2018/.*

Double The Donation. "Nonprofit Fundraising Statistics [Updated for 2020]." Accessed on May 26, 2020. *https://doublethedonation.com/tips/matching-grant-resources/nonprofit-fundraising-statistics/.*

Federal Election Commission. "Statistical Summary of 18-Month Campaign Activity of the 2017-2018 Election Cycle." Accessed May 26, 2020. *https://www.fec.gov/updates/statistical-summary-18-month-campaign-activity-2017-2018-election-cycle/.*

Ingraham, Christopher. "America's top fears: Public speaking, heights and bugs." The Washington Post, October 30, 2015. *https://www.washingtonpost.com/news/wonk/wp/2014/10/30/clowns-are-twice-as-scary-to-democrats-as-they-are-to-republicans/.*

Shin, Laura. "The Money Taboo: Why It Exists, Who It Benefits, And How To Navigate It," Forbes, April 14, 2015. *https://www.forbes.com/sites/laurashin/2015/04/14/the-money-taboo-why-it-exists-who-it-benefits-and-how-to-navigate-it/#4cb0adb02f62.*

CHAPTER 1 — THE FUNDRAISING FALL

Mind Tools. "The Conscious Competence Ladder." Accessed May 26, 2020. *https://www.mindtools.com/pages/article/newISS_96.htm.*

CHAPTER 2 — WHAT MAKES A GOOD FUNDRAISER?

Bankoff, Caroline. "How Selling Fax Machines Helped Make Spanx Inventor Sara Blakely a Billionaire." *New York Magazine*, October 13, 2016. *https://nymag.com/vindicated/2016/10/how-selling-fax-machines-helped-sara-blakely-invent-spanx.html.*

O'Reilly, Barbara. "Major Gifts Fundraising 101: It's Not About Us. It's About Them!" *The Non-Profit Marketing Blog*, December 17, 2015. *https://www.networkforgood.com/nonprofitblog/major-gifts-fundraising-101-its-not-about-us-its-about-them/.*

Tempel, Eugene, Timothy Seiler, and Dwight Burlingame. *Achieving Excellence in Fundraising.* New Jersey: John Wiley & Sons, 2016.

CHAPTER 3 — FEAR OF THE NO

Don, Geyea. "Obama's Loss May Have Aided White House Bid." *NPR*, September 19, 2007. *https://www.npr.org/templates/story/story.php?storyId=14502364.*

Great Schools Partnership. "GROWTH MINDSET." Accessed May 26, 2020. *https://www.edglossary.org/growth-mindset/#:~:text=Accordingpercent20topercent20Dweckpercent2Cpercent20per-*

centE2percent80percent9CInpercent20a,talentpercent20instead-percent20ofpercent20developingpercent20them..

Janny, Scott. "In 2000, a Streetwise Veteran Schooled a Bold Young Obama." *New York Times*, September 9, 2017. *https://www.nytimes.com/2007/09/09/us/politics/09obama.html.*

Josh, Bauerle. "Lessons in Overcoming Obstacles From Honda Motor Company." *CPA on Fire*. Accessed May 26, 2020. *https://cpaonfire.com/lessons-in-overcoming-obstacles-from-honda-motor-company/#:~:text=Howpercent20thepercent20company-percent20waspercent20only,ofpercent20theirpercent20size-percent20orpercent20industry..*

Startup.com LLC. "Startup Failure: It Happens. Let's Talk About It." Accessed May 26, 2020. *https://www.startups.com/library/expert-advice/startup-failure-lessons.*

CHAPTER 4 — FEAR OF THE ASK

Edwards, Heather. "Overcoming Fear: The Only Way Out is Through." *Psychology Today*, January 7, 2015. *https://www.psychologytoday.com/us/blog/the-intelligent-divorce/201501/overcoming-fear.*

Kopp, Wendy and Guy Raz. "Teach For America: Wendy Kopp." July 8, 2019. In *How I Built This*. Produced by NPR. Podcast, MP3 audio, 20:38. *https://www.npr.org/2017/11/29/556177643/teach-for-america-wendy-kopp.*

Sanders, Michael and Tamma, Francesca. "The science behind why people give money to charity." *The Guardian*, March 23, 2015. *https://www.theguardian.com/voluntary-sector-network/2015/mar/23/the-science-behind-why-people-give-money-to-charity*

CHAPTER 5 — FEAR OF THE AUDIENCE

Brene Brown, LLC. "Definitions." Accessed May 26, 2020. *https://brenebrown.com/definitions/.*

Carnegie, Dale. *How to Win Friends and Influence People.* New York: Pocket Books, 1981.

Cook, Gareth. "Why We Are Wired to Connect." *Scientific American*, October 22, 2013. *https://www.scientificamerican.com/article/why-we-are-wired-to-connect/.*

Blitz, Jeffrey, dir. *The Office.* Season 7, episode 10, "Search Committee." Aired May 9, 2011, on NBC. *https://www.netflix.com/title/70136120.*

CHAPTER 6 — GETTING STARTED

Atwood, Margaret E. (@MargaretAtwood). "Off to the Writing Burrow now . . . to face yet again the 'I don't know how to write' feeling . . . @ChuckWendig (It's never over)." Twitter, August 4, 2017, 10:36 p.m. *https://twitter.com/MargaretAtwood/status/893661928370917376.*

Ducharme, Jamie. "Psychologists Explain Why You Procrastinate—And How to Stop." *TIME*, June 29, 2018. *https://time.com/5322514/stop-procrastinating-tips/.*

Leak, Sophavatey. "Great Inventions from Procrastination." *UNICEF Cambodia*, September 6, 2016. *http://unicefcambodia.blogspot.com/2016/09/great-inventions-from-procrastination.html.*

Rautenbach, Anneke. "The Downside of Positive Thinking." *New York University*, January 14, 2015. *https://www.nyu.edu/about/news-publications/news/2015/january/the-downside-of-positive-thinking.html.*

Surowiecki, James. "LATER" *The New Yorker*, October 4, 2010. *https://www.newyorker.com/magazine/2010/10/11/later.*

Whitebourne, Susan Krauss. "5 Steps to Breaking Bad Habits." *Psychology Today*, August 23, 2011. *https://www.psychologytoday.com/us/blog/fulfillment-any-age/201108/5-steps-breaking-bad-habits.*

CHAPTER 7 — TAKING A RISK

Elkins, Kathleen. "J.K. Rowling 'Can't Stand' Following Rules—Here's What She Says to Do Instead If You Want to Succeed." *CNBC*, January 21, 2019. *https://www.cnbc.com/2019/01/18/jk-rowling-says-she-succeeded-by-breaking-rules-not-following-them.html.*

Harvard University. "J.K. Rowling Harvard Commencement Speech | Harvard University Commencement 2008." December 1, 2014. Video, 21:12. *https://www.youtube.com/watch?v=UibfDUPJAEU*

Scher, Bill. "4 ways Howard Dean changed American politics." *The Week*, June 21, 2013. *https://theweek.com/articles/462922/4-ways-howard-dean-changed-american-politics.*

Trippi, Joe. *The Revolution Will Not Be Televised.* New York: Regan Books, 2004.

CHAPTER 8 — GOALS

AchieveIt. "The History and Evolution of SMART Goals." Accessed May 26, 2020. *https://www.achieveit.com/resources/blog/the-history-and-evolution-of-smart-goals.*

Boss In Heels. "HOW TO SET GOALS ACCORDING TO 3 SUCCESSFUL ENTREPRENEURS." Accessed May 26, 2020.

https://www.bossinheels.com/how-to-set-goals-3-successful-entrepreneurs/.

Chowdhury, Madhuleena Roy. "The Science & Psychology Of Goal-Setting 101." *Positive Psychology*, December 2, 2020. *https://positivepsychology.com/goal-setting-psychology/.*

Robinson, Malia. "What Beyoncé Has Accomplished In 32 Years Is Mind-Blowing." *Business Insider*, September 4, 2013. *https://www.businessinsider.com/how-beyonce-became-famous-2013-9*

Weiss, Gabby, "GUIDE: The Basics of Fundraising for a Political Campaign." *NGPVAN*, September 10, 2018. *https://blog.ngpvan.com/political-campaign-fundraising-basics*

Whitely, Greg, dir. *Cheer.* Season 1, episode 3, "Blood, Sweat, and Tears." Aired January 8, 2020, on Netflix. *https://www.netflix.com/title/81039393.*

CHAPTER 9 — SELF AWARENESS

Ferris, Tim and Rice, Julie. "#372: Julie Rice — Co-Founding SoulCycle, Taming Anxiety, and Mastering Difficult Conversations." June 5, 2019. In *The Tim Ferris Show.* Produced by Tim Ferris. Podcast, MP3 audio, 43:48. *https://tim.blog/2019/05/30/julie-rice/.*

Formica, Michael. "Self-Blame: The Ultimate Emotional Abuse." *Psychology Today*, April 19, 2013. *https://www.psychologytoday.com/us/blog/enlightened-living/201304/self-blame-the-ultimate-emotional-abuse.*

Rosa, Christopher and Samantha Leach. "12 Famous Women on Facing—and Overcoming—Failure." *Glamour*, January 29, 2019. *https://www.glamour.com/story/famous-women-failure-quotes.*

CHAPTER 10 — WHERE DO WE GO FROM HERE?

Lambert, Nathaniel. "How Greater Challenges Help You Grow." *Psychology Today,* August 22, 2014. *https://www.psychologytoday.com/us/blog/strive-thrive/201408/how-greater-challenges-help-you-grow*

Weisel, Kimberly. "Only Crazy Obsession Could Have Built This $25 Million Ice Cream Empire." *Inc.*, December 4, 2014. *https://www.inc.com/kimberly-weisul/how-one-small-company-became-the-jedi-knights-of-ice-cream.html*

CHAPTER 11 — YOU ARE A FUNDRAISER

Bill of Rights Institute. "POLITICAL EFFICACY AND VOTER TURNOUT." Accessed May 26, 2020. *https://billofrightsinstitute.org/political-efficacy-voter-turnout/.*

Cherry, Kendra. "Self Efficacy and Why Believing in Yourself Matters." *VeryWell Mind*, May 17, 2020. *https://www.verywellmind.com/what-is-self-efficacy-2795954*

Good Therapy. "Military Resiliency Training." Accessed May 26, 2020. *https://www.goodtherapy.org/blog/military-resiliency-training.*

Houri, Charone. "A Hidden and Forgotten Story about Resilience." *Medium*, August 2, 2018. *https://medium.com/swlh/a-hidden-and-forgotten-story-about-resilience-cce0c1158946*

Ingraham, Christopher. "Low voter turnout is no accident, according to a ranking of the ease of voting in all 50 states." *Washington Post*, October 22, 2018. *https://www.washingtonpost.com/business/2018/10/22/low-voter-turnout-is-no-accident-according-ranking-ease-voting-all-states/*

Mandal, Ananya. "What Does Efficacy Mean?." *News Medical Life Sciences*, June 20, 2019. *https://www.news-medical.net/health/What-Does-Efficacy-Mean.aspx.*

Skills You Need. "Self-Awareness." Accessed May 26, 2020. *https://www.skillsyouneed.com/ps/self-awareness.html.*

CHAPTER 12 — CONCLUSION

Koshy, Cherian. "Fundraising as Risk Assessment and Management." *Association of Fundraising Professionals*, August 8, 2019. *https://afpglobal.org/fundraising-risk-assessment-and-management.*

Palmer, Barclay. "What Is the Difference Between Risk Tolerance and Risk Capacity?." *Investopedia*, February 27, 2020. *https://www.investopedia.com/ask/answers/08/difference-between-risk-tolerance-and-risk-capacity.asp.*

ACKNOWLEDGMENTS

I would like to acknowledge those who were early supporters of this book, without whom we couldn't have made it happen.

Amie Adams, Laura Allen, Rana Z. AlSaadi, Janet Arnold, Allie Atchley, Elena Bailey, Itay Balely, Elizabeth Z. Bartz, Christa Beal, Andy Blocker, Rebecca Brady, Alicia Brown, John Burrows, Brendan Byrne, Gregory Byrne, Patrick Byrne, Cindi Carney, Kevin Casey, Donna Cognac, Jennette Cheung, George Chipev, Joey Ciampa, Colin Craib, Emi Cummins, Emily Dindoffer, Elie Farhat, Laura Froelich, Richard Frohlichstein, Tonya Fulkerson, Abigail Gage, Christopher Gaginis, Rachel Gaglio, Matt Gardner, Marine Gassier, Meg Geiger, Julie Henson, Dave Hoffman, Joshua Hone, Joe Howard, Liz Hunger, Micaela Isler, Dani Jelensperger, Kafi Joseph, Kevin Karpay, Amanda Taylor Karpay, Amy Keys, Brian Killheffer, Alden Knowlton, Eric Koester, Ash Koirala, Gentry Lane, Susan Leslie, Shane Lieberman, Carolyn Lowry, Stean & Raissa, Manjiri Mannino Machak, Hannah

Malloy Peterson, Kathryn McDaniel, Erin McDonough, Lee Michel, Madalene Mielke, Helen Milby, Ben Miller, Carolyn Moore, Julia Moore, Sterling Morriss, Steven Moyo, Clark Nickell, Cady North, Dan O'Brien, Jennifer O'Reilly, Laurel O'Connor, Joseph Ottinger, Libby Pearson, Nate Pepe, Chris Postema, Judith Purvines, Lisa Ratner, Jenna Rekowski, Lindsey Rosenbaum, Brynn Ruriani, Jonathan Russo, Emily Seery, Marie Selvanadin, Sara Shaw, Mara Sloan, Brandy Stacks, Cara Stevens, Dan Tate, Amanda Taylor Karpay, Adron Vanderslice, Margaretta Veltri, Julie Vieburg, Brittany Wakefield, Deirdre Walsh, Gary Whidby, Benjamin White, Lori White, and Lawrence Young.

Made in the USA
Coppell, TX
21 September 2020